What people ar[e saying about]
Air Courie[r Bargains]

"Flying as a courier is the budget traveler's dream, for airfares as low as $99 — or even free. In exchange for giving up their baggage allowances, couriers are subsidized by businesses who use this method for overnight transportation of packages. Merely by occupying a seat in the plane, the courier acts as an agent accompanying the goods and the actual shipping and pickup is arranged at both ends of the trip by representatives of the sponsoring company. *The Insiders Guide To Air Courier Bargains* by Kelly Monaghan explain[s] the technique and list[s] companies through which arrangements can be made. The roster of company names is nearly identical [in other books], but Monaghan gives much more information about them and includes a destination and subject index."
Patty Campbell
Wilson Library Bulletin

✈ ✈ ✈ ✈

"An extraordinary value! The definitive book on the subject."
Arthur Frommer
Noted travel expert

✈ ✈ ✈ ✈

"The book is a best-seller."
New York Times

✈ ✈ ✈ ✈

"The most complete and up-to-date directory of air courier contacts."
Transitions Abroad

"Everything you need to know."
Travel & Leisure

✈ ✈ ✈ ✈

"Monaghan's book provides a wealth of information and an extended listing of agencies that arrange courier flights."
Ed Perkins, Editor
Consumer Reports Travel Letter

✈ ✈ ✈ ✈

"It's the best book out on the subject, and would probably be more useful to the job-hunting courier than any other book now in publication."
William C. Bates, President
International Association of Air Travel Couriers

✈ ✈ ✈ ✈

"There have been a number of books published on courier travel, but there is only one that's worth the money. That's *The Insiders Guide To Air Courier Bargains* by Kelly Monaghan. A comprehensive reference [and] a great tool."
The Shoestring Traveler

✈ ✈ ✈ ✈

"We all love to travel *and* save money. And no one does it better than Kelly Monaghan."
Kemp Miller
WFTR-AM

✈ ✈ ✈ ✈

"This book is a must read. No other book provides more information about this subject."
Mark Douglas
Travel Books Review

"This entertaining guide lays out the unromantic details of shepherding stuff — usually boring business documents — to exotic places. It's an excellent way to see the world on a shoe-string budget."
Linda Morgan
The Millennium Whole Earth Catalog

✈ ✈ ✈ ✈

"[There are] other air courier guides. The difference: This one's actually readable — personable as well as practical."
Pamela Robin Brandt
New York Daily News

✈ ✈ ✈ ✈

"At last, here's the complete guide to traveling as a courier."
Travel Books Worldwide

✈ ✈ ✈ ✈

"It's not hard to find books that tell you how to fly 'free' as a courier, but the best book on the subject is *Air Courier Bargains*. This is the only one I've seen where the author lays out absolutely everything you need to know about the prospects of flying for a reduced fare as a courier. If you're looking for a book that will take you by the hand, explain everything you need to know and then tell you where to go to find one of these travel bargains, this is the one."
Jack Reber
San Diego Union-Tribune

Also by Kelly Monaghan

Orlando's OTHER Theme Parks:
What To Do When You've Done Disney

Home-Based Travel Agent:
How To Cash In On The Exciting
NEW World Of Travel Marketing
(formerly titled *Part-Time Travel Agent*)

The Intrepid Traveler's Complete Desk Reference
(co-author)

A Shopper's Guide To Independent Agent Opportunities

Consolidators: Air Travel's Bargain Basement

Air Courier Bargains

Air Courier Bargains

How to travel world-wide for next to nothing

by
Kelly Monaghan

✈

Air Courier Bargains
✈ ✈ ✈
How To Travel World-Wide
For Next To Nothing

Published by:
The Intrepid Traveler
Post Office Box 438
New York, NY 10034, USA
http://www.intrepidtraveler.com

Copyright © 1999 by Kelly Monaghan
Seventh Edition
Printed in Canada
Book Jacket: FUSZION Art + Design

Library of Congress Catalog Card Number: 98-72668

ISBN: 1-887140-08-5

ACKNOWLEDGEMENTS

Thanks is due to the many courier companies and their representatives who have given so generously of their time in helping to update this edition. Special thanks is due to Sharon Frederick and Ron Byrd for their efforts on my behalf in Bangkok and Singapore and to Niall Monaghan for his assistance in Japan. And finally, a very special thank you to my loving wife, who smiles understandingly whenever I grab my carry-on and take off for far-flung corners of the globe.

— KM

PLEASE NOTE

Although the author and the publisher have made every effort to insure the completeness and accuracy of this guide, we assume no responsibility for omissions, inaccuracies, errors, or inconsistencies that may appear. Any slights of people or organizations are unintentional.

It must be understood that the listings in this guide in no way constitute an endorsement or guarantee on the part of the author or publisher. All readers who deal with the courier companies listed herein do so at their own risk.

Flying as a freelance courier involves a contractual relationship between the courier and the courier company. This book is sold with the understanding that neither the author nor the publisher are engaged in rendering legal or other professional advice. If legal or other expert assistance is required, the reader should consult with a competent professional.

The author and The Intrepid Traveler shall have neither liability nor responsibility to any person or entity with respect to any loss or damage caused, or alleged to be caused, directly or indirectly, by the information contained herein.

Table of Contents

About the Author

KELLY MONAGHAN is a New York-based business
and travel writer. In addition to *Air Courier Bargains,* he is the
author of *Home-Based Travel Agent,* which won a Recognition
and Achievement Award from the Outside Sales Support Network, a professional organization of independent travel agents.
He is also author of *Orlando's OTHER Theme Parks: What To Do
When You've Done Disney.* As a corporate screenwriter, he has
won a Cine Golden Eagle, a Telly, and both Gold and Silver
Screen awards from the International Film and Video Festival.
He speaks widely on the subjects of air courier travel and how
to set up a home-based travel marketing business.

Chapter One

Introduction

I pulled up my collar and smiled. I was on my way to London. In coach, yes, but certainly not as a mere tourist. I was an air courier!

Call me a romantic, but the very words — air courier — filled me with anticipation. As I strode purposefully into the terminal, I could hear Peter Lorre whispering to me from *Casablanca*. "Letters of transit. Signed by General DeGaulle himself. Cannot be rescinded."

I slid into a phone booth. Following instructions to the letter, I dialed a number and asked for Vince. No last name. Just Vince. We couriers are a cagey bunch.

"I'll send someone right over," Vince assured me. "Name's Danny. Meet him at the cashier's desk opposite gate one. What are you wearing so I can tell him?"

I gave Vince the lowdown. Trench coat. (I told you I was a romantic.) White shirt. Blue tie. I began to regret I hadn't thought to wear a red carnation.

I lounged against the wall by the cashier's desk and surveyed the crowd. How many, I wondered, were on a secret mission like me? And what would Danny be like? A rotund Sidney Greenstreet or a suave Paul Henreid?

"Mr. Monaghan?" Another in a long line of illusions was shattered. Danny was a scrawny, unassuming teenager, hardly a character out of a Bogart film.

Danny handed me my ticket and got me checked in. He

15

gave me a large white plastic pouch emblazoned with the logo of a courier company. My letters of transit, I assumed.

"It's empty," I observed.

"Yeah. Hold it up when you come out of customs in London so they'll be able to identify you," Danny explained.

"What am I transporting?" I dared to ask.

"Tell you the truth, I don't know."

I settled into my seat in coach and looked around. Now that my trench coat was stowed in the overhead I looked like just another (sigh) tourist. "At least I'm on the aisle," I thought and closed my eyes.

I arrived in London wondering if I would be humiliated in customs as "my" checked luggage yielded up some guilty secret while drug-sniffing dogs yapped in pleasure. Instead I was waved through without so much as a glance.

I soon made contact with London's version of Danny. He addressed me in fluent Cockney and escorted me to a small warehouse-like building ringed with courier vans. After a short wait, I was informed that everything was in order and I was free to go. As I walked toward the tube station for my trip into London, I felt let down. This wasn't the last reel of *Casablanca*. No rolling fog on the tarmac. No Ingrid Bergman. No romance.

The truth was simply that flying as an air courier was a cut and dried business proposition that got me to London on short notice for a mere fraction of what it would have cost otherwise. And that, I decided, was good enough for me.

✈ ✈ ✈ ✈

Since that first flight to London, I have become an avid courier traveler. I have even discovered an element of "romance" in the process. It's not so much in the actual travel — which is not much different from the experience of the "tourists" sitting next to you. The real payoff, I have learned, is in the wonder-filled reaction of my friends.

"You did what?" they asked incredulously.

"I went trout fishing in Venezuela for a week," I replied casually. "In the high lakes, they have some real nice ten-pounders."

16

At first, I'd explain myself by adding, "Of course, it was dirt cheap. I went as an air courier. Only cost me $175." That, naturally, led to a cascade of questions.

"Air courier? $175? Round-trip? How did you manage that? Tell me about it. What were you doing, transporting drugs? Really? How can I do that?"

Eventually, I learned to keep my mouth shut. Partly, I admit, it was to avoid answering all the questions. But just between you and me, I enjoy letting people think that the $100 fare to Chile, the $200 to Singapore, the $99 to Brussels — all round-trips — had cost much, much more.

✈ ✈ ✈ ✈

I used to think that air courier travel was just for special people — like me! — but as I learned the ropes and met my fellow couriers, I learned that there are no hard and fast rules about who is traveling as a courier. The old saying, "it takes all kinds to make a world" is just as true about the air courier business.

Are you cut out to be an air courier? You may be if you are:

• **A student.** Or anyone else with time on their hands and not a lot of money. Students and other young people have a natural desire to see the world and the flexible schedules that let them take advantage of the opportunities offered by air courier travel. Graduate students can use courier flights to do on-the-spot research that might be impossible at full fare.

• **A senior citizen or retiree.** The 'golden years' need not mean a rocking chair on a quiet porch. Senior citizens are much sought after by courier companies. Their reputation for promptness and reliability makes them especially desirable. One gentleman on the West coast has seen much of the Orient thanks to low-cost courier fares. Why not stretch those retirement dollars and indulge your taste for world travel?

• **A freelancer.** If you work on a freelance basis, I don't have to tell you how difficult it is to plan vacations. Just when you hope to get away, a big project comes in. The air courier option actually works in favor of the freelancer.

17

Here's a perfect way to reward yourself when a block of time opens up in your schedule. And there's another bonus: The shorter the notice, the cheaper the fare. You can finish a project one day and fly out the next using the strategies revealed in *Air Courier Bargains*.

• **A teacher.** Many teachers looked forward to tax-deductible travel during the summer. That was before "tax simplification." But while the IRS has curtailed travel deductions for teachers, air courier fares are still low, low, low. If the new tax rules made you think you couldn't afford to travel abroad to hone your teaching skills, think again.

• **An entrepreneur.** Like the freelancer, the entrepreneur cannot plan vacations months in advance. But entrepreneurs often want to explore overseas markets and keep costs down.

Many importers find air courier travel a dollar-saving strategy for exploring new opportunities or keeping in close touch with existing suppliers. If you have a product line that can be exported, courier travel offers a cheap way of exploring new markets and visiting potential buyers.

• **A smart shopper.** Even if you don't need to pinch pennies, air courier travel can expand your travel horizons. After all, the $500 (or more!) you save on air fare can pay for that luxury hotel you've always wanted to stay in but thought you could never afford! Or the same amount of money you budgeted for a weekend getaway close to home could take you to Mexico for a week!

• **Adventurous.** Let's face it, "beating the system" is fun! Picking up the phone and saying, "I'm available. What's the next flight out?" can bring the kind of thrills that well-planned vacations never offer.

It really is possible to indulge your taste for world travel and pay one-half, one-third, even one-tenth the cost of regular coach fares. Sometimes it is even possible to fly for free.

This book tells you how.

Chapter Two

The Air Courier Business

Couriers, of one sort or another, have a long and proud history. The earliest use of the word in English, cited in the *Oxford English Dictionary*, occurs in Wyclif's *Chronicles* of 1382 — "Curours wenten with letters."

Not much has changed in the last 600 years. Today, couriers still "go with letters." But today the distances couriers cover are truly global, the demand for expedited delivery vastly increased, and the medieval runner has been replaced by the modern air courier, traveling coach on jet airplanes.

Historically, couriers were used for military and diplomatic communications. In 1579, it was recorded that the Pope was making use of "dayly curriers and postes." In the seventeenth century, every military command had its "courier at arms." Alexander Hamilton and the Duke of Wellington both mention their use of couriers.

Of course, the diplomatic and commercial interests of great nations often coincided and diplomats and diplomatic couriers, with the immunity from search they enjoyed, became conduits for merchants with connections in high places. "Eventually," says Lawrence Burtchaell, an Executive Director of the Air Courier Conference of America (ACCA), an industry group, "the diplomatic courier became a commercial courier carrying shipments for clients in pouches as his own baggage."

The advent of the airplane just added a new wrinkle to an already well-established business practice. Indeed, carrying letters and documents was one of the first commercial uses to which the new-fangled flying machine was put. Today, of course, this specialized form of expedited delivery is a major industry.

"Air couriers, as we understand the term today, began in the sixties," explains Burtchaell. "When we began, 99% of what we carried was documents. Ninety percent of the courier companies would not handle high value stuff because it was too dangerous — they had couriers who actually ended up in the river. So most of them refused to carry things like gold and jewelry. What they were taking were documents that had to move very rapidly. It was all based on time-sensitive material. The postal services were very bad, and they still are for that matter."

It remains the same today. High-value articles are handled by specialists like Brinks Air Courier, which uses highly trained, bonded couriers and has developed special procedures to insure the safe arrival of valuable cargo. Most air courier shipments are decidedly mundane. Time-sensitive materials, of little value to anyone other than the sender and receiver, are placed aboard regularly scheduled commercial airliners as passenger's baggage. They are accompanied on the flight by an individual — usually referred to in the industry as an "on-board courier" or simply "OBC" — who carries the paperwork for the shipment.

But why are on-board couriers needed at all? Can't things be sent air freight without needing someone to accompany the shipment?

Of course they can, but there are two factors which have combined to create a niche for the on-board courier in the air freight business.

The first is the airlines themselves. "There are only two ways you can get your material on an aircraft," explains the Vice President of Line Haul at one prominent courier firm. "With a passenger as excess baggage or as general cargo.

"With general cargo, you normally have a lock-out time of four or five hours prior to plane departure," he continues. That is the latest the airline will accept cargo for a particular flight. "Your material has to be manifested by the airline and consolidated with other shipments in those big silver containers you see being trundled around the airport.

"As a passenger, you can arrive less than sixty minutes before departure and, depending on the security of the airport you're at, get your material on the plane."

The differences continue at the other end of the journey. "When the plane lands, passengers' baggage comes off first," he notes. "Twenty or thirty minutes later, your baggage is whizzing around the carousel for you to pick it up.

"The containers come off second. Then they have to be towed to a cargo facility, where they are opened, broken down, and segregated on shelves so that when people come with their airbills to collect their material and clear it, the material will be available for them to do that.

"That normally takes — at an absolute minimum — three or four hours. And, more realistically, at airports like Heathrow [in London], with the volumes they're dealing with, twelve hours is the norm."

The result, this executive concludes, is being able to offer his customers two and a half- or three-day service instead of overnight delivery. And that's simply not good enough.

The other major factor in creating a need for on-board couriers is what one air courier company executive refers to as "that dinosaur, the customs official." Not only does cargo have to get off the plane, it has to be cleared through customs in the foreign country.

No matter how complex or archaic a country's customs regulations are — and according to Burtchaell some of them are truly bizarre — a basic distinction is made between passengers' baggage and regular air cargo.

Once again, the most important factor is time. "Courier companies are in the business of express delivery," explains a London courier company representative. "Much of the courier material is made up of documents, mail, computer software and so on that are urgently required elsewhere in the world. Couriers are required so that the material can be moved as check-in passenger baggage, which if otherwise sent as air cargo can take up to three days to clear."

International packages sent via regular air freight can sit in bonded airport warehouses for days before they clear customs I am told. This also increases the likelihood of pilferage or loss. The baggage of a passenger on a regularly scheduled flight, on the other hand, goes through customs as soon as the plane lands. Many companies are happy to pay the additional charges to use an on-board courier service and make sure their valuable papers and packages arrive as quickly and safely as possible, on a scheduled flight.

✈ ✈ ✈ ✈

Many companies offer clients overnight, world-wide shipment, and many companies list themselves in the Yellow Pages under "Air Courier Services." They range in size from global giants like Federal Express to local mom-and-pop operations.

The major players in the industry, like Federal Express and DHL, are vertically integrated. That is, their employee picks up your package at your office, transports it in their van to the airport, and puts it aboard their plane. When the plane lands at its foreign destination, their employees unload it, their representatives clear the package through customs and place it in one of their vans, and one of their employees hand-delivers it to the person to whom you have sent it. These companies seldom, if ever, have a need for on-board couriers — at least to major foreign destinations.

Very few of the other companies, regardless of their size, actually handle the nitty-gritty details of getting an overnight shipment onto a plane. Instead, they turn over the overseas packages they receive to someone else and take a cut of the fee for finding the customer.

Thus, many companies that bill themselves as "air courier" firms in the Yellow Pages actually turn over their expedited shipments to someone like Federal Express, which charges them wholesale rates for their shipments. Others turn to an air freight "wholesaler" like Halbart in New York. Very few so-called "air courier" companies are the real McCoy.

Air courier wholesalers deal strictly with the mechanics of expedited air shipments; their customers are other shippers and not the general public. They have specialized in the detailed business of finding the couriers, negotiating wholesale tariffs with the airlines based on volume, booking the flights to get the packages overseas, and coordinating the whole operation. Many of their employees are bonded and carry special identification that allows them "behind the scenes" access. Because of their close contact with airline and customs personnel, these companies can offer freight forwarders a valuable service by speeding shipments into and out of the airports they serve.

A typical shipment sent out by a wholesaler will contain pouches from several different courier companies. This is known as co-loading. When the shipment arrives at its destination, each pouch will be picked up by a representative authorized to receive it. Larger companies, like Airborne, may have their own representatives at either end. Smaller companies may have reciprocal arrangements; in other words, the shipment from Joe's Courier Company in New York will be picked up by Fred's Courier Company in London, and vice versa.

Another category of air courier is the "retailer." Retailers go into the market to solicit business and then handle the courier shipments themselves. World Courier in New York is an example of this type of operation. Typically, retailers deal with larger business customers who ship in volume and who prefer the special attention and extra level of reassurance a retailer can provide. They are not interested in the onesy-twosy type of business; Federal Express handles that. Retailers may also co-load pouches from other companies with their own shipments.

As you can see, while there are many "air couriers," there are relatively few companies that actually deal with on-board couriers — a situation which can be problematical for the budget traveler, as we shall see.

✈ ✈ ✈ ✈

Courier companies make their money on the difference between what they charge their customers to ship something overseas and their actual cost of shipping it. It works out something like this: A typical charge for the trans-Atlantic shipment of a one-pound "letter" is $25. It costs the courier company about $1 dollar in freight charges by the airline to send that letter across the ocean, based on their putting 16,000 pounds of freight on a specific flight each week. Pickup and delivery costs at either end add another $10. So far, the courier company is left with $14 in gross profit.

Out of that profit comes the related costs of shipping the letter — the envelope it's sent in, the airbill, manifesting, bagging, payroll, trucking, the on-board courier's ticket, and miscellaneous overhead — which costs approximately $5 or $6 per letter.

Added to this is corporate overhead — executive staff, middle management, marketing, sales, customer service, and so forth — which accounts for an additional $3 or $4 per letter.

That means that after all expenses, $4 to $6 is left over as pre-tax profit. This may have to be shared among several parties, with the company that picks the letter up, the wholesaler who ships it, and the company that delivers it on the other end each taking their share.

Other customer service or collection problems may eat into this profit. "It costs $15 just to raise an invoice and collect a debt," claims one courier company insider. "By the time we've finished costing out an individual express letter, we may have lost $20 on the movement. And the only way we can bring that back into profit is volume."

The volume can be impressive. I once arrived in New York as a courier accompanying 87 pouches, and one pouch can contain 70 to 100 pounds of cargo. And that was on one flight. Worldwide, there are scores of courier flights every day. On the London-New York axis alone there are something like 160 rotations each week. By any measure, air couriers are big business.

Obviously, courier companies have good reasons to want their customers to believe that they are operating under the thinnest possible margins in providing them with this valuable service. But I tend to agree with the assessment of ACCA's Burtchell.

24

"It's a very lucrative business," he says.

✈ ✈ ✈ ✈

A s we noted earlier, the need for on-board couriers arises from a need for expedited delivery, on the one hand, and the hide-bound attitudes of the airlines and customs on the other. "How can we ship it as passengers' baggage without a passenger?" asks the airline. "How can I clear it as passengers' baggage without a passenger?" asks the customs agent.

The air freight company sighs and looks around for a passenger. And every year they have to come up with thousands of them. Where do they all come from?

Some are full-time employees of the courier companies. In the case of a specialist company like Brinks, there's no other way to do it. You can't entrust a million dollars in diamonds to just anyone. Brinks' couriers, however, have other duties and don't spend their entire working lives on planes.

Some companies, that need on-board couriers only infrequently, will use their own employees. In these cases, courier travel can be a perk (or a hidden liability!) of employment. And some companies actually employ full-time couriers whose job it is to fly from Point A to Point B and back again in the shortest possible period of time. If you've set yourself the goal of reading every single one of the World's Great Books, this might be a job worth having. Otherwise, I find it hard to imagine a duller job.

For most companies involved in the courier business, having full-time couriers on their payroll is not a viable option. Instead, they look outside. Many, if not most, on-board couriers are "casual couriers," part-timers like me — or you! A "casual courier," as defined by IBC-Pacific in their courier instructions, is simply "a person who accompanies time-sensitive business cargo that is checked on board an aircraft as excess baggage."

It's a marriage of convenience. The courier company needs someone to sit in the seat and carry out the minimal duties of carrying the paperwork. Thousands of budget-conscious travelers, on the other hand, are looking for a cheap way to get overseas.

In the distant past (15 years or so), you could actually get paid to be a casual courier. "We used to employ people," says one courier rep with a hint of amazement in his voice. "They used to fly Club and we'd pay for their hotels and everything!"

Then the courier companies discovered that there were people who were more than happy to give up their checked luggage allotment for a free ticket. Then some clever person (may he burn in fires eternal!) figured out that they could charge couriers a fee and still get takers.

"We discovered we could do it," says one courier company official matter-of-factly. "The key to any business is to charge what the traffic will bear."

So today the courier company has an additional interest in seeking outside, freelance couriers — the courier can offset some of the expense of the ticket.

✈ ✈ ✈ ✈

I am fascinated by the connotations the word "courier" has taken on in the popular imagination. For some, it conjures up visions of someone with a trench coat buttoned up to here with a leather briefcase handcuffed to their wrist. Others, who have obviously watched one episode too many of *Miami Vice*, cannot hear the word "courier" without thinking "drugs."

Once you begin traveling as an air courier, I can virtually guarantee that your friends will start asking whether or not you're transporting something at least mildly suspect — especially if you tell them how little you paid for your ticket.

The fact of the matter is that the air courier business is just as mundane as any other. It goes on day in, day out, year after year. It has well-established, cut-and-dried procedures that are carried out to the letter, with a high priority placed on safety and legality.

Would-be couriers can take comfort in the knowledge that the airlines require the courier companies to invest in extremely expensive x-ray machines to screen every pouch that's put aboard their planes. Customs, for its part, knows that smugglers are unlikely to send contraband through a channel in which the sender and recipient are so well identified.

It is also worth noting that the courier system has been designed to protect the courier company from the courier. That's why the courier never handles the shipment itself. Once the courier has had the cargo in his or her personal control for any length of time, the courier company cannot guarantee that the shipment hasn't been tampered with. The courier company is more interested in preventing theft than foiling drug smuggling on the part of the courier, but the very design of their system serves to remove suspicion from the courier.

"We have found contraband in these shipments," says U.S. Customs official Bob Fischler, "but percentage-wise it's infinitesimal. And in any seizure we made, it was obvious to us that the on-board courier had nothing to do with it." In fact, at New York's JFK and at London's Heathrow airports, because of the sheer volume of courier shipments, all courier pouches go to a central location for clearance. The courier has usually been dismissed before customs physically inspects the shipments.

✈ ✈ ✈ ✈

For as long as I've been traveling as a courier, people have been predicting the imminent demise of the courier business — at least from the standpoint of the freelance on-board courier.

"The fax machine will put an end to the need for couriers," was one theory. Yet the fax seems to have had little impact. For one thing, objects cannot be faxed. Many businesses are reluctant to fax signed contracts, except for informational purposes. And once a document reaches a certain length, it's cheaper to send it by courier than to fax it. Fax technology may, in fact, have increased awareness in the business community of the importance of getting things back and forth in a timely fashion and actually helped the courier business.

A more likely reason for courier flights to dry up is simple economics and the changing patterns of business. For any given courier run there will be a tonnage figure at which the route becomes profitable. In other words, if you can ship "x" number of tons of expedited cargo to Athens you will make money. Once the tonnage slips below that figure, the route will cease to be worthwhile and cargo will be shipped by another, less timely, method. "If they don't have enough weight — and it simply comes down to literal weight — then they can't afford to [use a courier]," says Julie Weinberg of Now Voyager in New York. "They have to send it without purchasing an actual plane ticket."

That's what has happened in recent years, not only to Athens but to Oslo as well. The air courier companies in New York found there was not enough demand to justify keeping the service open.

But while some routes close down, others open up. Beijing is now a destination from New York and Los Angeles; you can also fly to Johannesburg from New York, and there are the perennial predictions that we will soon see service to Moscow and other Eastern European destinations. And there are now flights from London to South America.

Of greater impact to the would-be courier are efforts to circumvent the air freight stumbling blocks that gave rise to the need for couriers in the first place. Some airlines have made a pitch for courier business by instituting special categories of air freight that will receive expedited handling. Australian customs, for one, has recognized the special realities of international business and begun providing expedited clearance. One result is that courier flights to Australia have declined — although they haven't disappeared altogether. Apparently, there is a perception in the marketplace that on-board couriers add an extra layer of service and accountability to expedited shipments.

While some courier runs may now be closed to the freelance on-board courier, there are still thousands of flights each year which need ordinary people like you and me to serve as couriers.

Chapter Three

Getting Started

M any people who are interested in traveling internationally as air couriers begin by picking up the trusty Yellow Pages and looking under the "Air Courier Services" listing. It sounds logical, but they are making a fundamental mistake.

The companies that have themselves listed as "Air Courier Services" in the Yellow Pages are not looking for people who want to travel cheap. They are looking for people or companies that want to ship time-sensitive papers, packages, or commodities overseas. Most of these companies are not true air couriers but what are known in the industry as "forwarders." They get the business and then "contract it out" to other companies that handle the actual air courier part of the transaction.

Moreover, these companies tend to be very poor sources of information about flying as a courier. For one thing, the people answering the phone may have absolutely no idea what happens to the packages they accept for shipment. For another, these companies have a vested interest in obscuring their mode of operation.

It all has to do with image. A memorable television commercial for DHL offers a perfect illustration of what the shippers in the industry want you to think of them: A DHL van is seen speeding through the air, passing an airliner in flight. Part of the message is speed. But DHL is also pushing the idea that, once you place your valuable package in their van, it stays there until it is delivered on the other side of the ocean. Regardless of how they really operate, all freight companies want to convey this idea of total door-to-door service.

That's why when you ask about being a courier they will say things like, "We use our own people," or "We have special arrangements with the airlines," or "We don't reveal that information." Nor are they likely to refer you elsewhere — other companies are, after all, their competition.

After calling dozens of companies, only to be told that they don't use freelance couriers, never have, never will, and don't know anyone who does, you will start to think that these rumors you've heard about super low-cost fares are a fantasy — either that, or someone's lying to you. Neither is true. Just remember that most of the companies listed in the Yellow Pages want to hear from people willing to pay a premium fee to ship important packages and not people who want to pay very little to ship themselves.

The "International Air Courier Directory" in Part II of *Air Courier Bargains* will save you hours of fruitless phoning to companies that don't want to hear from you and may be rude when you reach them.

✈ ✈ ✈ ✈

The first thing the would-be courier needs is a passport. Amazingly enough, ninety percent of Americans don't have one! If you don't already have a passport, don't think you can wait until you have booked a flight to apply for one. Most courier companies will ask you to prove that you have a passport before they'll give you a ticket. Some require you to provide them with a photocopy. I keep on hand several photocopies of the two pages of my passport that have my photo and personal information. That way I can present a photocopy or send one through the mail to assure the courier company that I have a valid passport. It's not a bad idea to have a photocopy in any case. If your passport is ever lost or stolen, having a photocopy can speed up the process of getting it replaced.

Generally speaking, nationality is no bar to courier travel, just so long as your papers are in order. In other words, you do not have to be an American citizen to fly as an air courier through an American air courier company, although some have different requirements for those holding non-U.S. passports. (See the "International Air Courier Directory" for details.) Courier companies in Canada and the United Kingdom assure me that Americans can take advantage of their courier flights. I have flown as a courier on flights outside the United States and had no problems whatsoever.

If you will be traveling to a country that requires a visa — Australia, for example — you must make your own arrangements and prove to the courier company that you have the required documentation. Often, the courier company will alert you that a visa is required but the responsibility is yours, so it's wise to double-check. It is a simple matter to check on visa requirements by calling the embassy or consulate of the country involved.

At this writing, countries requiring a visa for U.S. citizens are Australia, Brazil, China, and Honduras. Others, like Mexico and Venezuela, require documentation ("tourist cards") issued on arrival. You should also be aware that, even when your courier destination doesn't require a visa, the country next-door might. For example, it's a simple matter to fly as a courier to Bangkok and catch a cheap flight to Vietnam. But Vietnam requires a visa, which can take several days to obtain in Bangkok. As a rule, it's easier to get a visa in your home country than in a third country or at the border (which may be impossible).

Another thing to watch out for is length of stay. Most, if not all, countries that require no visa for short stays, will require them for longer stays. The definition of a "short stay" differs from country to country, but most define it as longer than the typical courier turnaround time. However, if you get one of the occasional courier flights that allow you to stay for six months or a year, you may very well need a visa. Always check! Even the friendliest countries can get a bit huffy when they discover you've overstayed your welcome.

For more information on getting passports and visas, consult *The Intrepid Traveler's Complete Desk Reference*, which I co-authored with Sally Scanlon. The *Desk Reference* is available from

The Intrepid Traveler, P.O. Box 438, New York, NY 10034, for $16.95, plus $3.50 shipping and handling. The book includes detailed information on visa requirements for all foreign countries and scores of sources of free tourist information about all the courier destinations listed in this book.

Passport in hand, you are ready to take your first courier trip. But to where? It helps to have a general awareness of where you can fly as a courier. As I noted earlier, the existence of a courier run between two cities is a function of demand, which in turn results from business patterns. If there is sufficient commerce between two cities or countries to make courier service economically viable, then it is more than likely that a courier company will attempt to tap that market.

From the United States, you can reach every continent except Antarctica as a courier. Far and away the most available destination is London, with flights from New York, Miami, Chicago, San Francisco, and Los Angeles. Otherwise, you will most likely find certain destinations available only from certain gateways: Europe from New York, South America from Miami, and the Orient from Vancouver, San Francisco, and Los Angeles.

From London, there is a different pattern, reflecting different patterns of commerce. A great many cities in the United States are available from London, while relatively few destinations on the European continent are offered. Because of the short distances involved, most courier flights to the continent from London are handled by employees who go and come on the same day. Flights to Africa, however, where England maintains close commercial ties to its former colonies, are available and there are once again a few flights to South America.

Other factors influence the availability of courier flights. For example, customs regulations in some countries are so strict that courier companies are forced to use professional, bonded couriers if they wish to do business in those countries. Also, customs duties are sometimes assessed according to the passport held by the courier, with nationals of the destination country enjoying an advantage; thus, courier opportunities are denied those of other nationalities. To cite another example, recent changes in Australian customs policies, making it easier to send expedited air cargo without an on-board courier have resulted in the decline (but not the disappearance) of courier slots to destinations like Sydney.

As you may have guessed by now, courier travel is an international phenomenon. Clearing customs, obviously, is not a consideration when you are shipping parcels from New York to Los Angeles. Nonetheless, every once in a while courier slots are available between New York and LA, as well as between LA and Miami. Here's how it worked in the past:

A niche in the market was created by the perceived unreliability of "over-the-counter" air freight offered by the airlines, on the one hand, and the relatively low cost of a passenger's ticket, on the other. A few entrepreneurial companies saw an opportunity to say to businesses that shipped in volume, "Look, send your stuff with us. We'll guarantee faster delivery than you're currently getting from the airlines and it will cost you less to boot." The entrepreneur would then buy a ticket and send the freight as excess passenger's baggage. An additional factor made this arrangement viable: The courier company could make these courier seats available to employees of its customer firms at no cost! It was a win-win solution all around.

According to Julie Weinberg of Now Voyager, which used to book these flights, economic realities closed the market niche. The airlines improved the reliability of their air freight and made the cost more competitive while the cost of a passenger's ticket rose. The courier runs ceased to be viable and the service ended. "If market conditions change, we may see these flights becoming available again," notes Weinberg. While you're waiting, Now Voyager (and a few other companies listed in this book) offer some attractive discounts on domestic, non-courier flights.

✈ ✈ ✈ ✈

Now you must decide where you want to go and when you want to go there. Making this decision is not quite so obvious as it may seem. There are three main ways to plan your air courier travel and the one you choose will determine your strategy in locating and booking a flight.

Option One: You can settle on a destination and approximate dates on which you would like to leave and return. Most of the companies listed in this guide will be most comfortable in dealing with you if you have a fairly firm idea of where and about when you want to go.

Option Two: Another approach is to choose a destination and fly there when a flight becomes available. That could be immediately or in three months. Most companies don't book flights more than three months in advance, although some have schedules stretching almost six months into the future. You may be forced into this choice with high-demand, low-availability destinations like Tel Aviv. You will have to monitor flight availability with the few companies that fly there and jump on the flight that best meets your schedule.

Option Three: Finally, you can choose a date or dates on which you will be available to travel and pick from the destinations available at the time. The sooner you book, the wider selection you will have. The longer you wait, the more likely you will be to find a bargain fare.

Once you have decided which strategy will work best for you, your next step is to get in touch with a courier contact that offers flights to the destination or on the dates of your choice. You can either deal directly with a courier company or use one of the various booking agencies that serve as middlemen in the courier industry.

I would recommend that, all things being equal, beginners use the booking agents, especially in New York. There are several reasons for this:

- One-stop shopping. Many booking agents offer more destinations than any one of the individual courier companies they represent.
- The booking agents are used to dealing with beginners. Part of what they get paid for is patiently explaining what courier travel is all about and helping you through the process.
- Getting information can be easier. The booking agent doesn't make money unless you book a

flight; so, in theory, he or she has a certain incentive to give you as much information as you need to make a decision and book a flight. The harried air courier operator, on the other hand, may know that the demand for seats is high enough to ensure that he'll get the couriers he needs, even if he doesn't take time to answer your questions.

- Sometimes it's the only way. In some instances, the courier company designates an agency as its sole representative. In other situations, you may not know which company to call directly for a flight to a city you want. The booking agents make it their business to monitor the industry and locate new opportunities for their customers.

- Some offer additional services that are not available from the courier companies. Some booking agencies also function as travel agents and can book you onto a flight that will get you to your courier flight. Also, the booking agencies that used to specialize exclusively in courier flights are branching out into other bargain travel niches, offering charter flights and special fares from the airlines.

The only real negative of dealing with a booking agent is the fee that some of them charge. In the case of Now Voyager, in New York, currently the only agency charging a fee, the amount is large enough ($50 annually) to make you think twice. If you fly only once a year to a $199 destination, you have instantly increased the effective cost of your flight by 25 percent! Of course, the more you fly, the less of an issue the registration fee becomes. Also the "year" is determined by when you book a flight not when you actually fly. So you can book a flight the day before your membership expires and depart two months later.

Whatever the disadvantages, the booking agents have their place. Even though I now consider myself to be an air courier veteran, I still use booking agents. One reason is their level of service. Now Voyager, for example, has a recorded message listing currently available flights and fares. (See the "International Air Courier Directory," page 93, for complete details.)

35

Naturally enough, the time may come when you will want or have to deal directly with the air courier companies themselves. There are a number of reasons for this:

- It may be the only way to get where you want to go. The booking agencies don't always provide universal coverage. And sometimes you will find that none of the booking agencies have a flight open when you want to go but a wholesaler does.
- It's fun! There's no quicker or better way to feel like an air courier insider than to deal on a first-name basis with the courier companies themselves, talking the lingo and getting inside information from the horse's mouth. Once you develop a personal relationship — and a track record for reliability and professionalism — you may even be able to move to the front of the line for special breaks such as last-minute bargain fares. (See Chapter Eight, "The Avid Courier," for more details.)
- You gain flexibility. If you travel frequently, as I do, you will soon find the limitations of the booking agents are "cramping your style." When you deal directly with the various air courier companies, as well as the booking agents, the whole world is accessible.
- It can be cheaper. Let's face it. We're talking bargain travel here, and the booking agents may mark up the fares, even if only a little bit. And if you don't have to pay a $50 fee, why do it?

If and when you decide to deal directly with an air courier company, you can simply use the "International Air Courier Directory" in Part II of this book to put yourself in touch with the companies that travel where you want to go.

Once you have an idea of where you want to go, when you want to go there, and the strategy you are going to use to get there, it's time to book your flight and take off. In the next chapter, I will walk you through the entire process, from the first phone call to your safe return home.

Chapter Four

How Air Courier Travel Works

E very air courier company has slightly different procedures but, in most cases, you can expect your air courier journey to unfold along these lines:

Step 1: Booking your flight

I have yet to come across a courier company or booking agent that won't let you book a flight by phone. Simply call and say, "Hi. I'd like to go to Rio in June. What's available," and they'll tell you. In many respects, it's just like booking through any travel agent — with one important difference:

The courier company wants to lock in that booking as quickly as possible, to assure themselves that they have a courier for that flight. That means you will have to pay for your trip as soon as possible. The seat is not officially yours until you pay and a delay in paying may mean losing the ticket.

Some companies will hold your reservation for a non-refundable deposit, pending full payment by a certain number of days before departure. If there is a comfortable length of time before the flight you may be able to pay by a personal check through the mail. More and more companies take credit cards (which may add several percent to the cost of your ticket). More common are policies that require payment in cash or by certified

37

check as soon as possible. That can mean showing up in person or sending payment by overnight mail. The "International Air Courier Directory" in Part II will help you determine which companies have which policies.

Once you have booked and secured a flight, you will most likely be asked to sign a contract. At this time, the company will make sure that you meet the minimum requirements (are 18 or 21 years of age, have a valid passport, don't have a spiked, day-glo hair-do and safety pins through your cheeks, and so forth). Sometimes all the contract-signing can be handled by fax. In some cases, you won't be asked to sign anything until you are being checked aboard your flight. We'll talk more about what you are agreeing to in these contracts in Chapter Seven, "Your Rights and Responsibilities."

Step 2: Boarding your flight

It's important to remember that, in the words of IBC, "you are not buying a ticket, but a trip." Even though your name may be on it, the ticket, technically, belongs to the air courier company. It's a subtle distinction that gives the courier company the right to "bump" you from the flight at the last minute. It does happen, but very, very infrequently.

Another result is that you will not receive the actual ticket until shortly before the flight. The day before the flight, you will most likely be required to check in by phone; they want to make sure you're still "on" for the trip. On the day of the flight, well before your scheduled departure time (two or three hours), you will meet a representative of the courier company at a pre-arranged location in the airport — or, less frequently, at the courier company's offices. Some companies will ask you to phone in when you get to the airline terminal.

Arriving at the airport with no ticket, often with rather vague instructions on where to meet someone you have never laid eyes on, is a new experience for most travelers. Frankly it can be a little nerve-wracking.

I once called American Airlines the day of a courier flight to see if I could have my AAdvantage number entered into their computer only to be told that my reservation had been canceled.

A call to the courier company brought reassurance that everything would be all right — as, indeed, it was.

Another common occurrence is to show up on time for your rendezvous with the courier rep only to be kept waiting for an hour or more. I now make it a point to bring with me the phone number of the courier company so I can call in if the rep is too long overdue. They always show up it seems. Any delays are caused by wanting to wait until the last possible minute to get as much cargo checked in as possible. So far — knock wood — I have never been left in the lurch at the airport and I have never heard of this happening to any other courier.

When the courier company rep arrives, you will be handed a one-way ticket to your destination, a sealed envelope, or "pouch," containing the cargo manifests for the shipment you will accompany, and a sheet of instructions telling you what to do for the return flight. Of these three items, the only one you are certain to receive is the ticket. Many companies have developed systems for getting their shipment through without entrusting the manifest to the on-board courier. And on some runs, you will be "coming back empty," that is you will have no courier duties on the return trip and, hence, need do nothing more than show up for and board the return flight.

The courier company representative will make sure that you are booked on the flight and get your boarding pass. In some cases, the rep will leave you in a waiting area and go deal with the ticket agents without you having to be present. At the very least, the courier company representative will be at your elbow as you go through the check-in procedure.

The same is true of the shipment you are accompanying. Many times you will never see the shipment you are accompanying; other times, the courier company rep will check in the pouches at the same time you are checked in. Several times I've watched burly cargo handlers drag large, heavy, corrugated plastic bags full of smaller parcels to the weighing machine at the airline counter, while I stood by. I have watched even larger loads being retrieved at my destinations (usually in the Far East). The point is, you will never be asked to physically manhandle the cargo yourself. You may be given the airline luggage check stubs for the courier shipment. If so, you will have to surrender them to the courier representative at your destination.

You will most likely be given something to help you identify yourself to the rep at the other end. One English company asks you to fill out a short questionnaire describing your dress and physical appearance; this is then faxed to the receiving company. Some companies issue their couriers with colored lapel pins or laminated, clip-on plastic ID tags, similar to those worn by airport personnel. Another courier company gives its on-board couriers a pin-on button that says, "COURIER. WHERE'S THE SHIP'S OFFICE?" (The ship's office is a term, dating from the times when most international cargo traveled by sea, that refers to the customs office.) I have even been given a sticker with the words "On-Board Courier" in Chinese. Generally, your manifest envelope will serve as your identification. These are usually large, white, plastic envelopes with the courier company name or "ON-BOARD COURIER POUCH" emblazoned on them.

Your major responsibility en route is to keep the manifests, the baggage claim stubs, and your instruction sheet safe and secure about your person. Hardly an onerous task.

Step 3: Arriving at your destination

When you arrive at your destination, you will be met by another representative of the air courier company. You may have been instructed to hold up the envelope containing the manifests as you leave the customs area to identify you to the person meeting your flight. Sometimes you will be given a phone number to call when you have cleared through customs. (Usually you will breeze through customs by following the "Nothing To Declare" signs.)

Once you make contact with the receiving courier company, you will be asked to wait — in the customs area of the terminal or in a building elsewhere on the airport grounds — while the courier company representative walks the paperwork and the checked baggage through the customs process. Once that's done, you'll be free to leave.

In my experience, this has been a hassle-free experience. I

have, however, seen other couriers who were not so lucky. While I was leaving after a five-minute wait at the courier shed in London, a courier from an earlier flight was fuming that he'd been kept waiting for hours with no explanation of the cause of the delay. On other trips to London, I haven't even been required to go to the customs shed; the rep simply asked where they could get in touch with me if they had to and let me go.

Once through customs, you are on your own, free to do and see as you please until the return flight. Depending on your destination, you may be asked to provide the courier company with a local contact number; the name of a hotel will usually suffice. Some companies like you to keep them apprised of your movements while there; in Singapore, for example, they tend to like to be informed if you will be leaving Singapore to travel to neighboring countries.

Step 4: Returning home

I have found that one of the most important documents I carry as a courier is the instruction sheet for my return flight. By all means, keep this document in a safe place. I copy the key information — return flight number and date, contact name, and phone numbers — onto several different pieces of paper to stash in various wallets and shirt pockets, just in case.

Usually, you will be asked to check in by phone with the local office of the air courier company several days before your return flight to confirm your flight and pick up any last minute instructions or changes in plan. In some countries, this can be a challenge, especially if you are not in the city in which the office is located. Believe me, you will complain far less about American phone companies once you have tried repeatedly and unsuccessfully to make a long distance call from a provincial city to the capital of a foreign country. Plan accordingly.

And don't forget to call or think it's just a formality that can be skipped. I have had flight times switched at the last minute. So always remember to check in. At the very least, failure to check in will earn a black mark by your name in the courier company's records.

On the day of your return flight, the arrangements are a

mirror image of the routine on the flight out — meet the representative at the airport, receive the manifests, if any, get checked in, receive your ticket, board the flight, meet the representative back in New York, or Los Angeles, or London. Most courier company reps will speak English, but you cannot always expect your foreign contact to speak, let alone be fluent in, English, especially in Latin America. A few pleasantries in the local language will come in handy. Fortunately, unless you have some problem, the procedure is so cut-and-dried that not being able to speak the language won't be a handicap. Also, if there is likely to be a language barrier, the courier company may very well provide you with bilingual materials. I have been given instructions and explanations in Japanese, Chinese, and Thai on various courier trips.

That's all there is to it. Considering how much you save on your fare, it's extremely well paid "employment."

✈ ✈ ✈ ✈

Can things go wrong? Of course they can, but they're the same problems that plague any other air traveler — delayed or canceled flights, overbookings, missed connections, and so forth.

Sometimes the glitches in a courier trip can be more interesting than inconvenient. David Bogartz had just such an experience on a trip to Oslo. "The representative meeting me there asked me to help him take the freight off the conveyor belt," he told me. "Being a nice guy, I couldn't say no, so together we dragged the bags out to the sidewalk. I could see through the plastic shells that the contents were Airborne Express packages. I wonder what the Airborne customers would think if they knew a computer programmer from Cambridge, Mass., had been dragging them across Fornebu Airport?"

On other occasions, the glitches can be more irksome. "I was going from Los Angeles to Singapore," recalls long-time courier George Sprague. "I was dropping off some baggage in

Seoul and then going on. Now normally, you hand the claim checks to [the courier company's] representative and he takes care of everything. In Seoul, it's a little different; in Seoul, the courier is responsible for getting the stuff through customs and then handing it over to the representative of the courier company's ground agent in Seoul.

"So it's Sunday night, it's winter, it's ten degrees below zero, I'm dressed for Singapore, I have 2,000 pounds of baggage, and the people who were supposed to meet me never showed up. Of course, they close Seoul airport at midnight and I have no place to put the baggage and no hotel. They were supposed to take me into town and put me up in a hotel.

"So I got customs to let me throw all the stuff back in the baggage area and I got my own hotel. I had all the tickets, so the next morning I caught my flight to Singapore and they didn't get their baggage in time." In spite of the hassle, George remains philosophical. "Screwups are possible," he notes.

Sometimes, the glitches can be downright dreadful. On rare occasions, the courier company will exercise its right under the contract and "bump" you from a flight. Sometimes they will want to accommodate a "VIP" with a free trip. That may not sound like a good reason to the courier, but it really doesn't matter since the courier company doesn't have to give you a reason. In a case like this, the courier is entitled to a complete refund of the courier fare. Any other expenses the courier might have incurred in getting to the gateway city will not be reimbursed. Fortunately, disasters like this are extremely rare.

On the other hand, the "problems" can sometimes be downright wonderful. Journalist Lee Solomon claims to have "the best courier story ever," and she just may be right. On her very first courier experience she booked a last-minute flight via the old Pan Am from New York to Frankfurt. The $150 fare was good enough but things quickly got better.

Courier companies like to be the last to check baggage for a flight. That way they can accommodate last-minute packages. On Lee's flight, she and a courier for another company weren't put on the flight until the economy section had completely filled. The result was that they were both bumped up to First Class.

While sipping champagne over the Atlantic, Lee was handed a scratch-off game ticket as part of Pan Am's fiftieth anniversary celebration.

"I won a free round-trip to anywhere in the world," Lee recalls. "Then, when I went to India on my free trip, they credited my frequent flyer mileage twice which meant that, with the mileage I got for going to Frankfurt, I was eligible for another free trip which I'm going to use to go to Africa. I wound up getting three trips, all for $150!"

Chapter Five

How Cheap Is Cheap?

The big attraction of traveling as an air courier, of course, is the tremendous discounts off the regular coach fares that come as part of the territory. The ticketed price of my first round-trip to London, which I described earlier, was $920; I paid just $250 and I booked the flight less than a week in advance. Of course, if I had booked well in advance for a super-saver fare I might have been able to do better than $920, but no airline, to my knowledge, was offering a $250 trip to London.

Charter fares tend to be more competitive with courier travel but are still priced higher, sometimes much higher, than the fares cited in this guide. What's more, charters are notoriously unreliable. Courier flights, however, are on regularly scheduled airlines. Even in the unlikely event that a flight is canceled, your ticket guarantees you passage on the next available flight out.

To give you an idea of what you can expect to save as a courier, you will find, on the next page, a chart listing flights and fares offered out of New York a few years ago, by one booking agent, in the middle of the summer, when fares were at their highest. Courier fares (and the 'regular' fares with which I compare them here) have risen a bit since then, and some destinations may no longer be available, but the principles remain the same.

In this listing, the "Date" column gives the *next* available flight, not the only flight available. In other words, the next flight to Amsterdam doesn't leave until the 27th of the month, but there may also be flights available on the 28th and 30th, as well as

DATE: July 14th

Destination	Date	Length of Stay	Fare
Amsterdam	7/27	1 week	$399
Brussels	8/4	1 week	$399
Buenos Aires	7/25	8 days	$399
Caracas	8/14	1 week	$175
Copenhagen	7/17	1 week	$199
Frankfurt	7/27	1 week	$399
Hong Kong	9/6	1 week to 30 days	$599
London	8/28	1 week	$350
London (from Houston)	7/26	up to 30 days	$375
Madrid	7/16	1 week	$150
Mexico City	7/25	1 week	$99
Mexico City	7/24	up to 3 months	$125
Milan	9/13	2 weeks	$399
Paris	7/19	2 weeks	$199
Rio	9/26	8 days	$399

Rome	9/4	8 days	$399
Santiago	8/15	13 days	$399
Singapore	N/A		
Stockholm	8/22	1 week	$299
Tokyo	N/A		

on several days in August.

This listing offers several impressive bargains. Madrid, at $150 round-trip, has been marked down from an earlier $399 fare. The reason? Check the dates; the flight leaves in two days. Even in the off-season, the generally available courier fares to Madrid are $299. Compare this to the $1,520 unrestricted coach fare you'd have to pay if you wanted to fly on the spur of the moment. That means this discounted courier flight is one-tenth the regular coach fare. Even with a 14-day advance purchase, with restrictions, the cheapest flight to Madrid would set you back $776 for a mid-week departure. So, flying as a courier, you're paying one-fifth (or 19.33%) of the cheapest fare.

Other bargain flights leaving in a few days are Copenhagen at $199 (down from $299), and Paris, a super bargain, at $199 for two weeks (down from $399). Another eye-opener on this list is the Mexico City fares. The fare had been running at $125 for a one-week stay. Here a one-week stay is $99 and a three-month stay is available for $125.

Even at "full" fares, courier travel offers significant savings. The Milan and Rome fares listed above correspond to Alitalia's cheapest fares for the same dates of $870 and $920 respectively. So even the highest fares you will pay as a courier on these routes are less than half what you could get from an airline. Or, for the mathematically minded, 46% and 43% respectively.

While we're at it, the above list also illustrates some other aspects of courier travel. The earliest flight available on the date listed was two days away; the latest "next available flight" was over ten weeks away. That's fairly typical of the industry, regardless of where you book your flights, although some flights can be booked as much as three months in advance.

Another thing you'll notice is that not all the destinations usually offered by this booking agent were available on this particular day. It's impossible to predict, much less guarantee, what will be available through any air courier contact when you call. Of course, you might be able to call another booking agent or an air courier company directly and find additional flights or better fares. As an example, while this booking agent was offering $399 flights to Milan, it was possible to find a $300 fare through a retailer.

Perhaps most important to the avid traveler is the fact that, on this particular date (and this doesn't change throughout the year), a wide variety of destinations and departure dates was available. Whether you want to leave quickly to wherever the Fates may dictate or want to be choosy and wait for the "right" destination, you will always be able to book a flight and still save hundreds of dollars — money that can be better spent doing what you want to do where you want to do it.

✈ ✈ ✈ ✈

In some respects, courier fares directly mirror standard air fares. That is, they tend to be higher during the summer and during holiday periods and cheaper during the so-called off-season. In one important respect, however, courier fares behave precisely the opposite of those offered by the airlines.

The farther away the flight date the better the deal you get on a "regular" fare from the airlines. As the flight date approaches, the few special promotional seats being sold at attractive "come-on" prices get filled. Next the 21- or 14-day advance purchase dates pass by. Finally, if you are forced to fly at short notice, the airlines sock it to you with their "unrestricted" coach fares, which can be truly astronomical, especially if you are not used to being forced to pay them.

For couriers the opposite is true. When the flight is still months away, the courier company will charge what they think the traffic will bear. As the flight date approaches, however, they begin to get nervous. The airlines can send a plane out with empty seats but the courier company has only one seat to fill and fill it they must. Within a week or two of flight time, the fares begin to drop.

So, if you can travel on the spur of the moment (and aren't too fussy about the destination), you can have the best of all possible worlds. As it gets closer to flight time, most companies lower the fare dramatically. My wife and I flew to Chile for $100 apiece round-trip. I flew from San Francisco to Bangkok for $148. I have seen Copenhagen for $50, London and Brussels for $99, and Buenos Aires for $199. And remember, those are round-trip fares! Times of international turmoil, like the Gulf War, are another harbinger of bargain fares. During that period you could find $99 round-trip fares to much of Europe and in some cases could even book a month or more in advance. Times being what they are, the same sort of situation could arise again.

But wait! It gets better. When it gets really close to flight time, the courier companies begin to get desperate. I had the opportunity to grab a flight from San Francisco to Singapore for free. Unfortunately, I couldn't leave that quickly and had to "settle" for the $148 trip to Bangkok I mentioned a little earlier. Various New York companies have given away trips to Hong Kong, Milan, and Buenos Aires. Jupiter Air, in San Francisco, and IBC-Pacific, in Los Angeles, are courier companies that will sometimes waive the fare for the last-minute traveler who helps them out of a bind. Obviously, because of the short fuse on last-minute bargains, they require that you be in or close to the city of departure.

In the "International Air Courier Directory" in Part II of this book, I alert you to those companies that have established procedures for alerting you to last-minute bargain fares and free flights, but the same principle applies to any courier company. If a courier isn't available for a flight, the cargo still has to go, and the owner of the company may not be as eager to go to Hong Kong or Rio as you or I.

Just because a flight is last-minute does not invariably mean that it will be free. Some companies seem to have firm policies on always charging something, no matter how short-notice the trip. You can always hold out for a lower fare or no fare, of course. The courier company may have other people on its list, however, and know that if you won't pay the price they ask, the next person they call, or the next, will.

If you are flexible as to your destination, I wouldn't worry about finding a bargain flight at the last minute — at least from New York. I regularly monitor the availability of flights. The longest time lag I have found between the date I call and the date of the next available flight is three days. In such a situation, don't hesitate to suggest a lower fare if it hasn't already been lowered.

You will find more on the subject of last-minute flights and bargain fares in Chapter Eight, "The Avid Courier."

✈ ✈ ✈ ✈

A ll talk of "free" courier flights should be taken with just a grain of salt. Just as there's no such thing as a free lunch, there's no such thing as an absolutely free courier trip. At the very least you will have to pay the applicable departure taxes (see below). Which is another way of saying that you will never travel for the fare the courier companies quote you.

One "hidden" cost has already been mentioned — the fees some booking agents charge. If you pay $50 annually and fly twice you have added $25 to the cost of each flight. When dealing with the already low cost of courier travel, this added expense is noticeable if not exactly onerous.

You may also incur some expenses in booking and paying for your flight. If you live in Las Vegas, Nevada, or Glasgow, Scotland, you will ring up some long distance telephone charges before you book your flight. If the time is short, you may find yourself paying to send and receive faxes of contracts. Banks will charge you for a certified check; money orders also cost money, although generally less than bank fees. Overnight mail or FedEx costs can also be a significant expense, especially if the courier fare is low.

Another fact of travel (and life in general) is taxes. The "good news" here is that you don't pay any more than anyone else on your flight. Nor do you pay any less. On a trip I took to Caracas for $175 round-trip, I paid a $16 departure tax in New York and another $11 departure tax in Caracas. That added just over 15% to the effective cost of my fare. Out of San Francisco to the Orient, the departure tax is $36.

Some companies require a refundable deposit of from $100 to $500 to "encourage" you to make the return flight. If you miss that flight — even if you have the best "excuse" in the world — you lose that deposit. Whenever I travel outside the city in which I land on a courier flight, I make it a steadfast policy to get back at least the day before my return flight. That way if I have any problems — canceled internal flights, lost traveler's checks, illness, or whatever — I have some built-in slack to maximize my chances of making that return flight.

Once you return, you will have to reclaim your deposit. This can often involve making a personal visit to the courier company or making cumbersome arrangements to reclaim your money through the mail. However, some companies (like Jupiter) simply mail your deposit shortly after you return; you don't even have to call them.

Even if you make your return flight and get your deposit back, you lose the "opportunity value" of your money — that is, the interest you'd have earned if you'd left it in your savings account. If you used a money order (a common form of payment), you also paid a dollar or two in fees. Instead, see if you can put your deposit on a credit card slip; they only submit the bill if you forfeit your deposit. Or write them a check, which they only deposit if you default. (Yes, yes, I know this is picky stuff, but if you're not interested in saving money, why are you reading this book?)

Some companies will encourage you, once they have your deposit, to leave it with them. That way, they argue, you won't have to worry about making the deposit on your next flight. You will have to decide whether this small convenience is worth giving the company a long-term, interest-free loan. If you're like me, inertia can play a role too. I left a return deposit sitting with a courier company on the theory that I'd have use for it in the not-too-far-distant future. That was years ago — I've just never gotten around to using it because I've been flying with other companies. By now I'd be too embarrassed to ask for it.

Then, of course, there is the always inflated cost of getting to the airport. For those of you who may be leaving from New York, let me pass along the following low-cost method for getting from Manhattan to Kennedy Airport (JFK).

Take the Rockaway bound "A" train to the Howard Beach/JFK stop. Be careful! One version of the "A" train goes to Lefferts Boulevard. You may also take the "C" train between 6:00 a.m. and 9:00 p.m. Sometimes (after midnight, for example) you will have to switch from the "A" to the "H" train at Euclid Avenue for service to the Howard Beach/JFK stop. Once on the "A" train it's a good idea to ask the conductor or a passenger to make sure. And, yes, New Yorkers can be both friendly and helpful! At the Howard Beach stop you can board a free 24-hour shuttle service to the JFK terminals. Total fare: $1.50.

Since you will most likely only be toting carry-on baggage, this alternative over a taxi ($30 or more) or the bus (about $13) is well worth it. Budget at least two hours from midtown Manhattan to make the trip.

Another "extra" (but not necessarily inevitable) cost of courier travel is excess baggage, which I will discuss in more detail in the next chapter.

✈ ✈ ✈ ✈

Courier companies are not travel agents. They provide only your transportation from a gateway city to and from the destination you have chosen. If you don't live in or near one of the "gateway" cities listed in the "International Air Courier Directory," you must find some way of getting there for your flight. What you do and where you stay once you get to your destination are completely up to you. Don't expect any help from the courier company on booking land accommodations. You may want to turn to a travel agent for help; just be aware of the fact that the agent may not react kindly to the news that you have already booked your flight.

For those of you who do not live in or near a gateway city,

the additional cost of transportation is a genuine concern. Fortunately, there are a number of strategies you can use to keep your in-country costs down. One option is to plan your courier travel around a business trip to a gateway city. That way, you will be able to deduct the cost of the domestic travel from your income tax.

Or, in the spirit of ultra-low-cost travel you may want to look into a "drive-away" to get you to your port of embarkation. Check your Yellow Pages under "Automobile Transporters and Drive-Away Companies" for outfits that will let you drive a car that needs to be delivered where you are going. The cities from which courier flights leave are popular destinations and you may be able to make the trip for little more than the cost of gas.

If you don't have the time to drive, you can either plan far enough in advance to qualify for advance-purchase discount fares or seek out some of the low-cost domestic air fare alternatives.

Bear in mind, too, that a growing number of courier booking agencies are branching out into the travel agent arena. Some offer discounted tickets to get couriers to gateway cities. Others have offered hotel packages in the past and are willing to help couriers with hotel arrangements. My guess is that we will see more of this sort of thing in the future.

While it is also generally true that the courier company (as opposed to the booking agency) cannot help you get from Kansas City to a flight that leaves from Los Angeles or Miami, Halbart, the New York wholesaler, boasts an in-house travel agency that has been very helpful in booking couriers on connecting flights into New York.

Another option is to dip into your reserve of frequent flyer miles to get a free round-trip ticket to a gateway city. Anyone who travels on business is enrolled in at least one airline program. Increasingly, you don't even have to fly to earn mileage credit.

American Airlines, for example, offers a number of ways to earn frequent flyer mileage credit without ever boarding a plane. If you use MCI for your long-distance telephone calls, you can enroll in a program that ties your long-distance bill into American's AAdvantage program. Call MCI at (800) 999-1909 to enroll and receive a 2,000 mile bonus just for signing up. Once you are registered, you will receive five AAdvantage miles for every dollar of long distance calls you make with MCI. Of course, if you don't use MCI, you can always switch.

You may also apply for a Visa or MasterCard from Citibank that gives you one mile of AAdvantage frequent flyer credit for each dollar you charge. The annual fee is $50, with the usual stiff annual interest. To apply by phone call (800) 359-4444.

Other Visa cards are offered by Alaska Airlines, America West, British Airways, Continental, Northwest, United, and USAirways. Continental also offers a MasterCard. Like the AAdvantage card, they all give one frequent flyer mile for every dollar charged.

Both American Express and Diners Club offer similar programs that have the additional advantage of allowing you to gain frequent flyer credit with a number of airlines. The American Express program lets you collect your frequent flyer miles from Continental, Delta, or Southwest. With Diner's Club, you can choose from Air Canada, America West, American, Continental, Delta, Mexicana, Northwest, Southwest, TWA, United, and USAirways.

Take a moment to reread the rules of the frequent flyer programs in which you are enrolled. Most of them have "partners" — hotels and car rental agencies — that allow you to accumulate additional mileage credit. Simply switching hotels on your domestic travels may earn you enough mileage to fly free to a courier gateway.

If you don't have enough of your own frequent flyer miles, consider buying someone else's. Check the classifieds in your local newspapers for people selling tickets or frequent flyer bonuses they can't use. *USA Today* regularly carries classified ads of companies that specialize in this business. Be careful, though. The airlines frown on this sort of thing and you run the risk of having your ticket cancelled if the airline finds out you're flying on someone else's miles.

✈ ✈ ✈ ✈

Consolidators, as they are known in the airline business, deserve special mention. In the simplest terms, a consolidator is a travel specialist who buys wholesale and sells below retail. In this case, the commodity being purchased is airplane seats. Consolidators buy large blocks of seats from the airlines at steep discounts. They then turn around and sell those seats to you or me at a price that is well below the ticket's "face value" but still high enough to earn them a profit.

When considering travel from a gateway city, consolidators can't come close to beating courier fares, as the following head-to-head comparison illustrates. All fares quoted are round-trip; where more than one fare is given, the consolidator quoted different fares for different airlines. The fares quoted are for the same dates of travel and lengths of stay.

Route	Courier	Consolidator
LA - Taipei	$300 (IBC)	$755 - $795 (Euro-Asia Express)
NY - Hong Kong	$450 (Now Voyager)	$890 (RMC)
NY - Milan	$200 (World)	$678 - $738 (Ameropa)
NY - London	$250 (Now Voyager)	$586 (Moment's Notice)
Miami - Rio	$350 (Air Facility)	$822 (25 Travel)
Chicago - Mex. City	$200 (Travel Hq.)	$327 - $343 (Mena)

If you're leaving from London, consolidator fares tend to be much more competitive with courier fares, although they are invariably higher by £50 to £100. If you live in England, you may find that the extra cost may be worth it to you, especially if the alternative is not making the trip. You will find a selection of British consolidators in Part II.

If you don't live near a gateway city, however, consolidators may offer an attractive alternative. For example, there are many flights from Orlando to Europe but no courier flights. A consolidator may be able to quote you a fare that is competitive with the cost of flying to New York or Miami to connect with a Europe-bound courier flight.

Generally speaking, consolidators offer overseas flights only, although a number deal with domestic flights as well. Those that do tend to offer long-haul routes (New York - LA, LA - Miami) or trips to Hawaii. In other words, if you live in Kansas City you'll have better luck asking a consolidator to get you to Hong Kong or Frankfurt than to Los Angeles or Miami.

I have written a whole book devoted to this important but little known corner of the air travel world. It is called *Consolidators — Air Travel's Bargain Basement,* and is available from The Intrepid Traveler for $7.95, plus $2.00 shipping. This book lists over 450 sources of cheap tickets throughout the United States and Canada. In most cases, you can book your tickets by phone and receive them in the mail.

Or you can take things a step further, as I have, and become a travel agent. It's remarkably easy — and perfectly legal — to set yourself up as a home-based travel agent. Once you do, you will be able to buy consolidator tickets for the rock-bottom "net fares" that are offered only to travel agents. You can use the tickets for yourself or resell them to friends or the general public.

I explain all the ins and outs of profiting from travel marketing in *Home-Based Travel Agent: How To Cash In On The Exciting NEW World Of Travel Marketing,* available for $29.95, plus $3.50 shipping and handling, from The Intrepid Traveler, P. O. Box 438, New York, NY 10034. For more information, visit The Intrepid Traveler's web site at http://www.IntrepidTraveler.com.

✈ ✈ ✈ ✈

56

Finally, you might want to keep an eye peeled for special deals and promotional fares available from the airlines themselves. I have never seen these fares match courier fares but sometimes they get close. For example, here were some deals being offered by various airlines not too long ago. Similar deals will be available as you read this.

- TWA was offering fares of $198 round-trip to various European cities for short stays on a limited number of dates.
- Icelandair was offering round-trips to Luxembourg from New York and Baltimore for $398 and from Orlando for $498, with a free rental car for a week (if two people traveled together).
- Virgin Atlantic was pushing a "Late Latesaver" fare from Boston to London for $179 one way or $368 round-trip, which would make it very competitive with a New York courier flight if you lived in or near Boston.

How do you find out about these special deals? Good question. It can be difficult. The daily paper is one source, but it takes an eagle eye and an immediate response to grab bargains before they sell out.

I subscribe to *Consumer Reports Travel Letter* and *Best Fares*, which alerts subscribers to opportunities like this. Trouble is, these promotional fares are often sold out before the newsletter arrives. However, *Best Fares* has a web site with up-to-the-second information for subscribers only.

If you have access to email and the Internet, there is another way to spot bargains. Visit the web sites of the growing number of airlines that offer weekly specials on undersold flights; there you will be able to sign up on-line to receive weekly email bulletins about budget fares. Most of the bargains offered are for domestic flights that leave at the weekend and return early the following week, but there are international flights as well.

Here are some web sites to visit:

American Airlines	http://www.americanair.com
Continental	http://www.flycontinental.com
Northwest	http://www.nwa.com

TWA	http://www.twa.com
USAirways	http://www.usair.com

Again, perhaps the best way to monitor the availability of specials like these is to set yourself up as a part-time, home-based travel agent. There are a number of publications published monthly, weekly, even twice weekly, which are available to travel agents for a very low price. In fact, some of the very best are free! These publications will keep you abreast of all the latest developments and trends in the travel industry — including fare wars, special deals, and introductory bargains.

Once you're plugged into the travel distribution system, you will be more likely to hear about it in time when a too-good-to-pass-up opportunity comes along.

Chapter Six

Tradeoffs

If it sounds too good to be true, it probably is. While that may be overstating the case a bit, there are some tradeoffs to air courier travel.

The biggest drawback, say most people, is the baggage limitation. A growing number of courier runs, especially to the Far East, allow one or two pieces of checked luggage. You also get a full luggage allotment on some courier flights to London out of New York and on virtually all courier flights out of London to the rest of the world. On most runs, however, the courier company still limits you to one piece of carry-on luggage, so if you haven't mastered the art of traveling light, courier travel may be a bit of a challenge.

Before I became an air courier, I was an inveterate over-packer — the sort of person who'd throw in a tuxedo "just in case." As it happened, I found the discipline of reducing all my travel needs to a single bag strangely liberating. I have now arrived at the point where I find I am still over-packing, even in just one carry-on bag!

Another "advantage" of traveling light is that, even on a one-week trip, you will most likely have to do laundry. Of course, you can send it out if you are staying in a hotel that offers laundry service. I prefer to do it myself. Going to the laundromat may be an unwelcome chore at home, but in Siena, Italy, where I learned some invaluable lessons about opening and closing times, it becomes an enjoyable cross-cultural adventure!

Actually, what constitutes "carry-on baggage" is a matter of constantly shifting definition. Some courier companies specify you may only take one bag, while others allow you two. The airlines, for their part, have their own definitions. The "standard" definition is one bag with combined dimensions (length, width, and height) that do not exceed 45 inches and that does not weigh more than 70 pounds. Generally, the less crowded the flight, the more you can get away with. The key factor is that whatever you lug aboard fit in the overhead or beneath your seat.

For years, I traveled with two bags — one a largish leather bag that just met the airlines' combined height, width, and length requirements, the other, a small, over-the-shoulder bag in which I carried camera, guide books, tickets, and so forth. I was never challenged and never found the combination a burden.

Then I discovered the Travelpro Rollaboard. It has spawned many imitators, but this is the original — the one that, not too long ago, you only saw being used by airline personnel. It's a nifty little black rectangular bag, just small enough to meet the carry-on limits, that comes with a set of wheels and a retractable handle, so you can wheel it along behind you.

Since I discovered it, I've field tested it over thousands of miles of European cobblestones and Asian alleyways and now won't take a courier flight without it. The Travelpro employs an ingenious two-tier packing mechanism and even comes with a removable section for a suit. I am constantly amazed at how much 'stuff' I can cram into it. For my money, it's the premier courier's bag.

If you absolutely can't stuff everything you need into one little bag, you might consider wearing several layers of clothing. Women, of course, have the option of carrying an oversized "purse" in addition to their regular carry-on allotment.

Another, often overlooked, strategy is to ask the courier company with the "carry-on only" policy if they'd be kind enough to let you check a bag. You may be pleasantly surprised. Couriers who have traveled with the company several times are more likely to be extended this courtesy than first-timers.

As a last resort, you can simply pack another bag and pay for "excess baggage." If you do this, make sure you check with the airline for the prices and procedures on the route you are flying before you get to the airport. Policies vary greatly from airline to airline and from route to route, in part due to regulations mandated by the country to which you will be flying. For example, on United's flight from New York to Caracas, you can check an "excess" bag of no greater than 100 inches in total dimensions and no greater than 100 pounds for $45. On United's New York to Brussels flight, however, they charge $90 for a bag not to exceed 62 inches in total dimensions or weigh more than 62 pounds.

Sometimes the problem is not what you want to take with you but what you want to carry back. If you plan on doing any heavy shopping, my advice would be to make as many arrangements as possible for shipping it back before you leave home. The embassy or consulate of the country in question will direct you to reputable shipping companies. Another good source of information about reputable shippers is the American Chamber of Commerce, which has offices in most major foreign cities.

And don't put off your shopping spree until the last minute. I once had to pass up some fabulous bargains in Mexico City because the merchant didn't ship to the United States and I had no time to make other arrangements.

Be aware, too, that on some courier runs you will be either going or returning "empty" — that is, there will be no courier pouches to accompany on one leg of the trip. Sometimes, this is a peculiarity of that particular route, other times it's simply the luck of the draw. If it's important to you, ask about it before your trip. If you know you'll be returning empty, you can plan on bringing a collapsible bag with you and loading up on goodies while overseas.

✈ ✈ ✈ ✈

Another drawback of courier travel is that you will most likely travel alone. Invariably, any given company has one courier seat on any given flight.

That does not mean that two people cannot plan on traveling together, as long as they are willing to be a little flexible. For example, Virgin's courier service out of New York to London has two flights each day, so you and a companion can leave and arrive only hours apart.

The more likely scenario is that you and your companion will book seats on succeeding days. Use the "International Air Courier Directory" to spot likely candidates for this arrangement. Or you can simply tell the courier company what you have in mind when you call. Companies that offer several flights a week are the most obvious choices. If they can swing it, they'll be more than happy to accommodate you. After all, they need to fill those seats.

Obviously, the farther in advance you book, the better your odds of booking on successive days. In my experience, courier companies and booking agents are regularly able to accommodate couples with this type of arrangement. Before you dismiss this strategy out of hand, consider the benefits. Most couples do not share all the same interests; there are invariably sights to see and things to do that appeal to one more than the other. This strategy gives each person some time on their own at the destination to use as they see fit, without worrying about boring their companion. When my wife and I went to Chile — for $100 each — we used this strategy and it worked out just fine.

If you simply can't bear to be separated, there are other options. With a little planning, you should have no trouble booking a super-saver fare for a companion on your courier flight.

It is also theoretically possible (although I've never tried it) to find two different courier companies with seats on the same flight or at least on the same day to the same destination. Your best chance for this kind of arrangement is on the heavily traveled London - New York corridor.

In general, however, air courier travel works best for the solo traveler. Which may not be as bad as it sounds. Even the most social among us sometimes has a need to get away by themselves. If you've been promising yourself that someday you'll "do" the Louvre, or if you want to go snorkeling on a tiny coral island in the Caribbean, or simply want to "stand silent on a peak in Darien," a courier flight may be just the ticket.

✈ ✈ ✈ ✈

I t is often said in the industry that the air courier must be flexible. Yet, paradoxically, you also lose flexibility. You must fit yourself into the company's schedule, not vice versa. While you can pick your destination, it is not always possible to pick your dates. And sometimes you can pick the date if you are willing to be "flexible" on the destination.

Once you book a flight, the dates are locked in. Most courier companies have fixed lengths of stay for each route. For them, it's purely a matter of convenience. It's a lot easier to keep things organized if you know that all couriers return in precisely one week, than if you have to juggle lengths of stay ranging from a few days to several months.

Other companies will offer flexible stays "up to 21 days" or "up to a month." That does not always mean that you can pick any length of stay within that time frame. More likely, your date of return will have to coincide with an available flight.

Some companies will try to accommodate requests. For example, if the usual stay at a particular destination is two weeks and someone wants to stay only one week, that might be arranged if someone else is willing to stay three. These special arrangements are rare, however.

The rigid length of stay requirements also mean that you can forget about changing your return date. You may fall in love with Paris or Rio but if you want to spend more time there, you'll have to plan another trip. Don't think you can talk the courier company into letting you stay an extra few days. Still, special circumstances do arise and — who knows — it may just be in the company's interests to have you stay an extra month. As with so much else in life, it never hurts to ask.

But in spite of the drawbacks — and there's no point pretending they don't exist — air courier travel, because of its very unpredictability, remains one of the few real adventures left in this age of homogenized travel. If you've never traveled on a whim, being an air courier will give you the experience of taking off at short notice to points unknown. If you've written off the Far East or South America as vacation destinations because they're just too far away and too expensive, air courier travel can make these exotic destinations suddenly affordable.

I especially recommend air courier travel to people who, like me once-upon-a-time, are inclined to plan their vacations down to the nth detail. Dropping everything after a job well done or at the tell-tale signs of burnout and saying, "The heck with it. I need a break," then picking up the phone and saying, "I'm ready to go. What's available?" is one of the most liberating experiences imaginable.

Try it. It's worked wonders for me. It can for you, too.

Chapter Seven

Your Rights and Responsibilities

The question I am asked most frequently about my courier travels is, "How do you know you're not transporting drugs?" It's gotten to be a bit of a joke.

The fact is that the courier business is as boring as most other businesses. Things get moved from Point A to Point B and if someone, somewhere along the line, slips some contraband into a shipment, it's certainly not your fault. As the folks at IBC told me, "The individual shipments are inspected prior to being manifested so that only legal commodities are being shipped."

It also helps to remember that most of the material you will be accompanying is being sent by companies with which the courier companies have long-standing business relationships. In the lingo of the airlines, these are "known shippers." It is relatively rare that a stranger to the courier company walks in with a single package to ship. In any event, all packages, suspicious or not, are x-rayed by the courier company before they are trucked to the airport.

The people in customs know this as well. In fact, I have received far less attention from American customs when arriving as a courier than I ever did when arriving as a regular "tourist." Also, the last time I returned from London, I carried a letter from the London courier firm stating in black and white that I had no personal responsibility for the contents of the shipment I was accompanying. Needless to say, I didn't have to flash it in self-defense.

In the unlikely event that some contraband does turn up in a shipment you are accompanying, the suspicion will fall not on you, not on the courier company, but on the person who sent the package originally. You probably wouldn't be inconvenienced in any case since you most likely would have left the airport long before any contraband was detected by the eagle-eyed customs inspectors.

The non-issue of drug smuggling aside, the fact remains that being a courier is a serious business that involves a contractual relationship between you and the company for which you are serving as a courier. Each of you has mutual obligations that are spelled out in the agreement you sign before traveling.

To state the obvious, I am not a lawyer and it is certainly not my intention to render any legal advice. This chapter contains only the ruminations of a layperson. Should you feel the need for legal counsel before embarking on a courier trip, by all means seek it. Just don't seek it here.

✈ ✈ ✈ ✈

One of the more curious aspects of courier travel is that the courier companies will insist (in the fine print of their contracts) that your ticket is free; then they turn around and cheerfully charge you for that "free" ticket. "The airplane passenger ticket to and/or from your courier destination is free of charge in consideration of your performance of JUPITER non-salaried on-board Courier duties," says Jupiter's contract.

But several paragraphs later the contract stipulates, "There is an administrative charge of _____ payable at the time the offer is accepted. The administrative charge serves to cover part of JUPITER's related administrative and operational expenses and is not charged by JUPITER as an agent for any airlines or as a ticket agent." The blank space is filled in with the amount of whatever "fare" you have agreed to pay for your Jupiter flight.

To the courier, the money paid to the courier company looks, feels, and acts like a fare. In the "International Air Courier Directory" in this book, I always refer to the fees charged as fares. To normal folks like you and me they are fares.

To the lawyers who draft the contracts, however, there is a crucial difference. In their efforts to protect their clients (the air courier companies) from every possible eventuality, the legal eagles have set things up in such a way that the courier never has the actual, technical, legal ownership of the ticket. The courier company always retains ownership and control of the actual ticket, even if it has your name written all over it.

This arrangement offers the courier companies the maximum flexibility. It enables them to change plans — or even cancel — at the last minute. Suppose, for example, that you have made arrangements with a courier company to be their courier on an American Airlines flight to London. Then, at the last minute, they get a large rush shipment from a major customer, too late to make the American flight. However, they can get the shipment on a later Air India flight. If the ticket was "yours," you could say, "Tough. I want to go on American and collect my frequent flyer miles. This late shipment is your problem."

The way the contract you signed is written enables the courier company to cancel the flight on American and put you on the later Air India flight, frequent flyer miles or no.

Another common contractual provision is confidentiality. Halbart's contract, for example, asks you to agree to the following statement: "I will not discuss with anyone Halbart's method of operation or names or lists of clients of which I may be aware, or which may be in my possession."

I suppose that could be interpreted to mean that you couldn't tell the person sitting next to you on the plane that you paid a fraction of the going rate for your ticket in exchange for acting as a courier, although most couriers I have spoken with tell me that bragging about the fare is one of the best things about courier travel.

According to Jonathon Steinberg, an international lawyer

who represents several air courier companies, the confidentiality clause is there to protect the companies from industrial espionage. If you traveled with a courier company on several trips, learned the ins and outs of their operation, picked up the names of some of their best customers, and then set up a courier company of your own, in direct competition, they would have some legal recourse.

✈ ✈ ✈ ✈

Can you collect frequent flyer mileage when you travel as a courier?

Yes and no.

The answer depends on who you talk to. Some courier companies will tell you that you can collect the mileage; they may even use that fact as an inducement for you to fly with them. Others will insist that it is impossible for couriers to collect frequent flyer credit.

Ultimately, whether you can collect frequent flyer miles is determined by the fare code attached to your ticket. As you may know, the seats on any given flight are sold at a bewildering variety of fares. Each of these fares is connected to a fare code, which in turn is connected to a long list of rules governing that fare — advance purchase requirements, days of the week on which it is valid, refund provisions (if any), and so forth.

Some fare codes for very low-priced tickets specify that no frequent flyer mileage will be awarded — on the apparent theory that the airline earns so little on the ticket that giving away frequent flyer miles does not make economic sense.

If you really want to get into the arcane world of playing the ticketing game, I will refer you to my book, *Home-Based Travel Agent: How To Cash In On The Exciting NEW World Of Travel Marketing,* which explains how to become a travel agent and cut your own deals with the airlines.

For the casual courier, however, my advice is simple: Always ask about frequent flyer mileage when you book your flight with the courier company. If they say "no," ask the airline when you check in for your flight. Very often, they will take your frequent flyer number, even though the courier company has told you you're not eligible. There could be any number of reasons for this: The courier company was mistaken, the ticketing agent didn't check the fare code or didn't know its restrictions, the computer doesn't cross-reference frequent flyer numbers and fare code restrictions, or some other reason.

It's happened to me. While checking in for a courier flight from London, for which I was told frequent flyer miles were unavailable, I handed my frequent flyer card to the ticketing agent. The courier company rep said, jokingly, that he thought the courier company should get the frequent flyer credit since, after all, it was the courier company that paid for the ticket. The ticketing agent disagreed. "It's the bloke what puts 'is bottom in the seat what gets the credit," he said. Amen.

Of course, sometimes you will be handed a ticket and boarding card that have the words "NO AIRLINES MILEAGE" stamped on them in big, bold letters. In these situations, I have always assumed that they really mean it and have not risked embarrassing myself and possibly alienating the courier company by asking for mileage anyway. But, who knows, maybe someone with a little more chutzpah than I could ask and receive.

I have been told that fare codes that specifically exclude frequent flyer miles are less common today and will be phased out completely in the near future. Lawyer Steinberg, a frequent courier himself, suggests that, whatever the situation, you always ask for your frequent flyer miles. "Airline regulations and codes are so complex and in such a state of flux," he notes, "that very often the person doing the ticketing doesn't know what's allowed and what isn't."

Upgrades of courier tickets are a related issue. In other words, if you have sufficient frequent flyer miles in your account, can you upgrade your courier ticket to Business or First Class? Some courier companies state that no upgrades are permissible on their tickets; others say nothing. Again, the answer depends on the fare code and the imponderables of airline policies and the efficiency with which they are applied. Another problem is the fact that you receive your ticket only minutes before flight time. As I mentioned before, it is possible to call the airline several days ahead of time (to request a special meal, say) only to find that they show no record of you being on the flight.

If you are interested in upgrades, my advice to you would be to follow the same guidelines outlined above. Ask. At the courier company. And at check in.

✈ ✈ ✈ ✈

Far and away the most important obligation you have as a courier is to be where you are supposed to be when you are supposed to be there. Carrying an envelope on an international flight is not exactly a job for a rocket scientist. However, making flight connections and following simple written instructions is something that, so I have been told, eludes a surprising number of would-be couriers.

Among the cardinal sins are missing flights or waltzing through customs without meeting the courier representative and turning over the manifest. Any such transgression means instant blacklisting by the courier company involved and perhaps by others as well.

In New York, for example, many courier companies turn over the job of handling incoming courier shipments to New York Air Courier Clearance (NYACC). A similar service is performed at London's Heathrow Airport by Courier Facilities Ltd. The people staffing these operations get so annoyed with less than responsible couriers that they are liable to spread the (bad) word among the companies they serve.

Sometimes, the payback can be more immediate.

A courier rep at Heathrow in London told me of a returning courier to New York who tried to avoid his responsibilities by telling the airline he had lost his ticket. Sure enough a check of the computer revealed a ticket in his name (paid for by the courier firm) and a new ticket was issued.

The courier rep, who was holding the real ticket, suspected

something was amiss when the courier didn't show up as pre-arranged. He asked the ticket agents if Jim Smith (not his real name) had checked in and was told, "Yeah, that's him over there."

The rep approached Smith, who admitted that he simply had wanted to save himself some time at customs in New York. The courier rep, predictably, was not amused. Jim Smith was now faced with a choice, lose his ticket and pay his own way home or complete his agreed-on mission as a courier. He chose the latter.

The London courier firm faxed a complete description of the offending courier to New York along with a few nasty suggestions about how to best handle the situation. The result: Jim Smith spent three long hours bottled up in customs before being released.

Another fairly common blunder is missing the return flight. Often this happens when the courier travels away from the destination city and does not budget time for unforeseen eventualities when making return arrangements. I know of couriers who booked a flight that would get them back in "plenty of time" to catch their returning courier flight, only to have the flight delayed, then cancelled. When they missed the return flight, they were surprised to find the courier company wasn't sympathetic.

It helps to remember that courier companies are in the freight business, not the tourist business. When you miss your return flight, you cause the courier company inconvenience, added expense, and a potential loss of reputation with its clients. It's no wonder they are not sympathetic. In these situations, the contract is on their side.

✈ ✈ ✈ ✈

When you get right down to it, there's not a lot to do as a courier. You are simply operating as a very small cog in a much larger operation. Everything has been done to make your job as foolproof as possible — not so much for your benefit as for the company's.

Once aboard, you are just another coach passenger. Your "job" as a courier earns you no special privileges or consideration

— although a courier from Wales told me that on a flight from London to Philadelphia he talked the cabin attendant into letting him sit next to the door in Club Class "since I was carrying urgent courier documents." (How do you say 'chutzpah' in Welsh?)

Still, small though your part is, it is important. Carrying out your part of the bargain promptly and efficiently will help you build a reputation that can pay off down the road in inside information and special deals. It will also help remind the courier companies that freelancers can be a valuable and valued part of their operation.

Fortunately, most people who fly as freelance, on-board couriers are solid citizens who take their courier duties seriously, even if it means some discomfort. The following story comes from a British courier who requested anonymity. He was on his first courier flight, from London to New York. Everything went smoothly, until he checked in for his return flight. Then came an announcement of a delay in the flight. Our courier picks up the tale:

"It was whilst I stood by the desk in the departure lounge that my problems began. I had thought it best to ask if I could phone [the courier company] to let them know about the delay. As I stood by the desk, waiting my turn to ask, a person with an official air appeared quickly by my side and said 'Courier?'

"Taken by surprise, I answered 'yes' and in my confusion allowed him to take the sheets of information that [the courier company] issues couriers and that gives telephone numbers in case of emergency. As he went to walk off with these I said, somewhat sternly, 'I'll keep the documentation,' and took a firm hold of them. For a split second we both held this sheet and my heart started to hammer. I thought he was not going to let go. 'We are both in the same business,' he said. 'I worked for [the airline] for 30 years and then I started playing around with this.' I kept a firm hold on the sheet as I asked him if he worked for [the courier company] but he zoomed off without, apparently, hearing me.

"After speaking to the desk staff, I found a wall to lean against and I saw this man again. He was in his sixties and reasonably smartly dressed in a brown sports jacket and trousers. He started to fiddle with one of the computer terminals at the desks and when an airport employee walked up to see what he was doing, he used the same attitude that he had used on me and the employee walked away. I was not so convinced and wondered if he was some type of con-man.

"Much later, on the way to the hotel, the airplane unfixable until the morning, I saw him again. He showed me a telex that he had sent out which advised his family that he would be late. I was impressed but still deeply suspicious. The following day the plane took off normally. I had noticed this man again. This time he was being questioned by a purser on why he was sitting in an upper class seat with an economy ticket. I was unable to hear his reply but I noted that he remained seated. The flight was uneventful and soon we were getting ready to land.

"As I reread [the courier company's] instructions I saw, with great apprehension, this man walking along the aisle. He was looking at each passenger and I knew, instinctively, that for some reason he was looking for me and I was right. He sat in the empty passenger seat next to me. Looking at me firmly he said 'I'll take all your manifests. I will be through customs before you.'

"Returning his firm look with what I hoped was one of my own, I said 'No, that's all right, thank you.'

"He gave me a look of surprise and hurt and said, 'You will be hanging about there all night. Give them to me. I know where to take them.'

"'That's quite all right, thank you. I have telephone numbers to ring should there be any problems.'

"'Look,' he said, 'You don't know when they will turn up. Where do you keep them? In your bag?'

"He nodded towards my holdall that I had placed on the other empty seat next to me. He was right; that is exactly where they were. My heart was pounding once more. I had no experience of this work and did not really know what to expect. Clearly though, I was responsible for these manifests and for the cargo that they represented.

"'Look,' I said. 'I don't know who you are from Adam and I have no authority to give these documents to anyone.'

"'One minute,' he said and with that he left.

"He had obviously gone for something which gave me

time to compose myself and to work the next bit out. I made certain that the zip was firmly closed on my bag and then, dismissing the fleeting thought that perhaps I should go and sit somewhere else as the action of a coward, I made up my mind that he would not take these documents off me.

"He returned and showed me a card with his photograph and the name of a company on it which seemed hardly like a ticket to take the manifests. The discussion, which was getting a little heated on both sides, continued until shortly before the landing when he returned to his seat.

"As I walked away from the plane I saw him hanging around and he waited for me to come alongside of him. I ignored him and went to collect my suitcase.

"The cargo doors had jammed on the plane so there was a delay before I was able to leave. The first person I saw, on leaving customs, was the [courier company] representative. With a relieved smile I handed him the manifests.

"'You would have saved us all a lot of trouble if you had given these to Les when he asked you,' he spat at me.

"'What a fool I would have looked if you were asking me for these and I told you that I had given them to a complete stranger on the plane,' I said.

"'He was an employee of [the airline] for thirty years,' I was told.

"'But I didn't know that,' I said.

"'I know him very well,' said the rep. It seemed pointless arguing, so I left.

"As a postnote, I did feel quite embarrassed over the incident but I have to say that I firmly believe, given the circumstances, that I acted correctly and until I am given detailed instructions that clearly specify that I am to part with these manifests to persons other than the courier representative I will act in exactly the same manner again. Much better a few people are upset than a consignment goes missing."

I agree completely and the courier company involved should have been pleased that (in the obvious absence of instructions from them to the contrary) this courier protected their paperwork so assiduously.

✈ ✈ ✈ ✈

There are some other points about professionalism that are part of the fine print of the contracts you sign that you should be aware of.

You are expected to dress neatly and conservatively. Now Voyager specifies jacket and tie for men while IBC makes a jacket optional. For women, Now Voyager stipulates "dress, suit, or other businesslike attire," and draws the line at "faded" blue jeans for either gender.

IBC says it tolerates jeans if they are "clean, pressed, and unfaded." However, they draw the line at "thongs, suggestive T-shirts, shorts, and unconventional hairstyles."

British Airways Travel Shops (BATS) is another company with fairly strict fashion standards. They prefer jacket and tie for men and, for women, a dress, blouse and skirt, or "smart trousers." Their courier information sheet goes on to warn, "You will be refused travel if you check in with denims, shorts, or trainers on."

On my early flights, I always dressed like a businessman but I noticed that the dress regulations seemed to be honored more in the breach than the observance. On one trip, I found myself waiting at customs with a Brazilian student wearing a faded t-shirt and shorts and a young woman from Britain in tattered jeans.

I suspect this happens because the courier company (which is usually represented by a fairly low-level employee) only gets to see what the courier is wearing a short time before the flight. It's probably easier to let it slide than to bar the courier from the flight and find a replacement.

I have now adopted a two-tier policy toward my courier wardrobe. If my activities at my destination will require a jacket and tie, I wear them on the flight. This not only meets the most stringent courier regulations but has the additional advantage of saving space in my carry-on luggage. Otherwise, I dress more casually but neatly and I have never had a problem. If you steer clear of blue jeans, t-shirts, shorts, and those dreadful "trainers," you shouldn't have any problems.

Another common provision in most courier contracts prohibits consuming alcohol before or during your flight. "The Freelance Courier agrees to consume no alcohol in flight," says the Now Voyager contract in no uncertain language. Another contract stipulates only that you maintain "a strictly professional and sober manner during the flights and thereafter until all of Courier's duties hereunder are fully discharged," which would seem to imply that you could drink just so long as you remained (or, at least, acted) sober. Jupiter's contract makes no mention of alcohol.

Certainly no one has ever given me a breathalyzer test when I arrived and I know other couriers who admit to imbibing en route. I suspect that the courier companies are most concerned about having a courier roll off a flight roaring drunk, thus complicating and delaying the customs process.

This suspicion was confirmed by a tale I was told recently of a woman who was serving as a courier on a flight from London to New York.

This particular flight kept passengers happy with an open bar. The lady in question proceeded to become quite drunk and rowdy, so much so that she had to be physically restrained by the attendants.

Unfortunately for the courier company that had put her on the plane, this flight was diverted from Kennedy to Newark. There are few situations in which the common sense of a courier can make a difference, but this was one of them. As it transpired, by the time the plane touched down at Newark, the courier in question was senseless and had to be wheeled off the flight — literally.

Fortunately for all concerned, she had been seated next to a courier for another company (who told this lurid tale) who explained the situation to the flight attendants and customs, was able to take charge of the situation, and looked after the now-abandoned courier shipment until the people who were picking it up made the long, inconvenient journey from JFK to Newark.

So be forewarned. If you do decide to indulge in flight, be discreet.

✈ ✈ ✈ ✈

I f you're like me, any discussion of contracts and legal responsibilities may leave you feeling slightly queasy. Lawyers are paid, a lawyer-friend once told me, to imagine all the horrible things that can possibly go wrong and then protect their clients against them.

The lawyers who draft these contracts for the courier companies are no exception. That is why courier contracts are liberally spiced with cheerful words like "loss or damage," "personal injuries," "cancellation," "accidents," and that all-time favorite, "death." They tend to be long on what the courier company can expect from you and short on what you can expect from the courier company.

In practice, courier travel is just as uneventful as "regular" travel. The worst-case scenarios envisioned by the courier contracts are unlikely to occur. And it might be noted that when you buy a regular airline ticket you are agreeing to page after page of fine print (in effect, a "contract") which severely limits your rights and recourse against the airline.

Nonetheless, the fact remains that a contract is a contract and flying as a courier obligates you to play by rules that are different from those that apply to other forms of air travel.

At a minimum, you should read the contracts carefully and make sure you understand and are comfortable with their provisions. If you have any questions or reservations, seek the advice of a competent professional.

To keep my lawyer happy, let me repeat that I am not of that noble profession and that nothing in this book should be construed as rendering legal advice. If you feel a need for such advice, hie thee to a law firm. And bring money.

✈ ✈ ✈ ✈

To end on a cheerier note, I will point out that couriers often enjoy an advantage not shared by other coach passengers. That is, they have someone who desperately wants to see them leave the country. Now.

The courier company wants to get its cargo overseas as quickly as possible. But what happens if the flight is canceled because of mechanical difficulties?

Most passengers will become the airline's guests overnight or cool their heels uncomfortably in the airport waiting for the problem to be fixed. And, as happened to the British courier who told the tale earlier, sometimes the courier will join them.

Other times, however, the courier company will get a ticket on another flight, on another airline, leaving that day so that their precious cargo can be delivered on time. Sure it costs them a little more but it might be worth it to them in long-term customer satisfaction. The courier, of course, benefits as well.

The same principle applies to overbooked flights. That's why I constantly hear reports of couriers being bumped — not off the plane but into First Class. In fact, I was giving a talk on courier travel recently and asked how many people had had this happen to them when they flew as couriers. Three hands went up.

Now if it would only happen to me!

Chapter Eight

The Avid Courier

For most people, courier travel is a sometime thing. It's a way to take an occasional holiday and nothing more. People like this may fly once every year or two. For others, courier travel becomes tantamount to a way of life. These are what I call "avid couriers."

The avid courier, in my experience, tends to fall into one of two broad categories: retirees and business travelers. For retired people, courier travel offers a perfect match — they have the time at their disposal, they can be completely flexible as to dates, and they are living, by and large, on a fixed income that makes the low cost of courier travel especially attractive.

George Sprague, a retired social worker for the county of San Diego, is a perfect example. He takes a minimum of three "vacations" a year and has visited Singapore, Bangkok, Tokyo, Seoul, Hong Kong, and Taipei as a courier. Most of the time he travels free by taking advantage of the need for last-minute couriers.

"If you book well in advance, you pay the advertised fare," he explains, "but I find out what flights they have going for a whole month. Then a day or two before the flight, I call them up and ask, 'Is this flight open?' If it's open, fine, I'll take it because I know it's going to be free."

Obviously, it doesn't work every time and this is where a retiree's time flexibility comes into play. "I may have to make a dozen calls before I get a flight," George notes, but his track record proves that, with a little perseverance, a free flight will be forthcoming. "They've even called me on two occasions and said, 'We've got a flight going and it's free if you want it.' So they obviously have my name on their computer and they go down the list and say, 'This guy's gone a lot, let's try him.'"

Other retirees will pick a favorite destination and plan on going when they can get there super-cheap. According to Tom Belmont of Halbart's Miami office, "We have people who call up and say, 'Look, I have a granddaughter at school in England. If you ever have something going for $100 or less, give me a call.'"

For business travelers, even if they can easily afford full fare and are at the platinum level in all the frequent flyer programs, the lure of courier fares can be hard to pass up. A perfect example is Jonathon Steinberg, the international lawyer with offices in London and New York. He travels back and forth as a courier eight to twelve times each year.

There are a number of factors that make courier travel a natural for the businessperson. First and foremost is cost. I have business interests in Europe that might never have come about without the ability to get back and forth cheaply. Courier flights offer an ideal way of exploring new markets or checking out potential suppliers — and any money saved on airfare goes directly to the bottom line. And since most business travelers are flying by themselves, the solo nature of courier flights is no liability whatsoever.

In this Chapter, I will discuss strategies and techniques you can use to join the ranks of avid couriers by establishing yourself as an asset for the various courier companies.

✈ ✈ ✈ ✈

The first step in becoming an avid courier is to get to know the industry and the people in it. This will tend to happen naturally as you take one courier trip after another. However, you can and should take the initiative.

When you travel as an air courier through a booking agent,

get to know the people you meet. While you are waiting for your flight, pass the time by asking the courier company rep a few "innocent" questions: What's the best way to deal directly with your company? Who should I ask for when I call? Where else do you fly to? Do you know any other companies I might call for courier flights? Can I get any special deals from your company if I can fly at the last minute?

You probably won't be able to ask every question you might have. You have to remember that, for the courier company, you are no more important — in fact, you're probably *less* important — than the paperwork that accompanies the shipment. Don't expect the reps to entertain you; they are not tour guides. I have discovered that the hallmark of the professional air courier is an air of calm self-assurance and asking too many "dumb" questions can blow the image.

Nonetheless, people are people and they tend to react positively to genuine interest in what they do. If you hit it off with a courier company rep, you can get some good, straight-from-the-shoulder information. And remember to *listen* to the answers you get. Make a special note of any jargon that's specific to the courier business. The more you know about how the business in general and specific companies in particular work, the easier it will be to deal direct. On the other hand, don't expect everyone you meet to be an industry expert. As in any other business, some of the reps you meet will know how to do their specific job — and nothing else.

Another good source of information is the person who meets you at customs on your return. This person may not represent a courier company at all. In New York, it's often a representative of New York Air Courier Clearance (NYACC). At London's Heathrow, it may be someone from Courier Facilities Ltd. These are not courier companies but clearing houses that handle the customs hassle for a number of different companies. Consequently, they can give you the latest information on who's still in business and where they fly to.

Yet another source of valuable information is your fellow couriers. Often you will find yourself hanging out at customs with one or two other couriers. Ask them who they're flying for and quiz them for tips on other companies they have flown for. Get their home addresses and keep in touch. Let them know that you would appreciate it if they could pass along any new information they might pick up on their travels.

✈ ✈ ✈ ✈

Anyone who intends to make courier travel a regular part of their lifestyle owes it to themselves to become a member of the International Association of Air Travel Couriers (IAATC). Despite its grand-sounding title, this Florida-based outfit is a straightforward, and rather homey, newsletter operation that will provide you with regular updates on the air courier scene.

The $45 annual membership fee ($80 for two years) brings you two newsletters published bi-monthly in alternating months. The *Air Courier Bulletin* is a no-frills pamphlet printed on newsprint. It contains regular updates on courier companies, their destinations, fares, and policies. It doesn't cover quite as many companies as I do in this book, but it covers most of them. I have found it to be, by and large, accurate and reliable, although given the nature of the ever-changing air courier industry they're bound to miss a few every now and again.

On alternate months you receive *The Shoestring Traveler*, a slickly produced 16-page newsletter that is a wonderful source of straightforward information and tips about how to continue your budget travel adventure once you step off your courier flight. You'll benefit, for example, from tales of how the editor traveled from Florida to Lisbon (via London) as a courier, getting a nuts-and-bolts introduction to the budget delights of Portugal into the bargain. Other recent articles covered surviving Rome on a budget and an overview of low-cost travel to Central America. There are also bits and pieces of news, humor, and ephemera of interest to the budget traveler, all served up in a light, breezy style. Even if you never travel outside your home town, *The Shoestring Traveler* makes for delightful fireside reading.

As a member, you can also get an "official" courier identification card, complete with a color photograph. In practical terms, it's probably about as "official" as your old Captain Midnight decoder ring but, what the heck, it's fun and it may just convince some skeptical types that you're a bona-fide courier professional!

A far more important benefit of membership, in my opinion, is IAATC's fax-on-demand service. By calling a special number at their Lake Worth, Florida, headquarters from your fax machine and punching in your personal access code, you can receive up-to-the-minute news of last-minute discounts, new routes, and non-courier travel bargains. You pay only for the call to Florida. It is also possible to retrieve this information via the Internet, making it even cheaper and more convenient. Of course, the information is never going to be as up-to-the-second as the information you get by calling the courier company directly, but at least it can point you in the right direction.

The International Association of Air Travel Couriers (IAATC)
International Features
8 South "J" Street
P.O. Box 1349
Lake Worth, FL 33460-1349
(561) 582-8320

✈ ✈ ✈ ✈

While you want to get to know the courier companies, your ultimate goal is to have them get to know you. "The secret of courier travel is to build up a relationship with these companies and show them that you're reliable," advises courier lawyer Jonathon Steinberg. "So that whenever there's a choice between using you or using someone else, you'll hope they'll always want to use you."

There's a theory that if you make casual contact with anyone three times, they will remember who you are. Put this theory to work as you set out to establish yourself as a reliable courier.

Make a note, mental or otherwise, of the names of all your contacts in the air courier business. This is a basic networking technique. Your goal is to get them to remember you as a reliable and professional courier. Being able to ask for the right person when you call or ask, "How's Jimmy doing?" gives you a leg up.

Another way to establish an identity with a courier company is to send a short thank-you note after each trip. Often, the instruction sheets and other materials you receive when you travel as a courier will alert you to the appropriate person to whom to address your note.

Here are some suggestions for making your notes most effective:

- Send your note to the head of the company if possible.
- Make a point to commend any of their employees who have been particularly friendly or helpful.
- You also might to want to drop subtle hints about how often you fly: "This was my fifth courier trip with you . . . "
- Type your note on business stationery if you have it. Otherwise, hand-write it neatly on personalized stationery.
- If you can fly at short notice, say so.

Steinberg suggests another way to win share of mind with the courier companies. "When I'm going across the Atlantic and a client is paying, I'll often call up [a courier company] and say 'Do you need a courier for tomorrow? I'm going over.'" He is, in effect, offering his services at no charge to the courier company and at no additional inconvenience to him. If the company has had a last-minute cancellation, an offer like this can be a life-saver. It's also possible that the company might find it useful to use Steinberg's ticket to ship some additional cargo. Even if the courier company can't take him up on the offer (which is the most likely scenario), he has further established himself as an asset to the company.

I should point out that an offer like this will be much more meaningful coming from someone the company knows well — like Steinberg — than from a stranger off the street. You may want to hold off using this ploy until you have established a track record with the company.

✈ ✈ ✈ ✈

A bove all, the would-be avid courier must estab- lish a reputation for complete and utter professional- ism and reliability.

"Look at it from their point of view," says Steinberg, refer- ring to the courier companies. "They're in a quandary. They've got to put people on planes. They've got to make sure those people are reliable. But they've got to put so many people on planes so often that there's no way they can ascertain whether all these people really are reliable. So what you have to do is show these people that you're someone they can do business with.

"And that's the important point," he stresses. "They've got to know who they can rely on. These guys have been stung a lot. People have a tendency, even when they've paid a couple of hun- dred dollars for the ticket and might lose it, not to show up for the flight. When someone doesn't show up for the flight, they've got to send their station manager out to England. Then they're without their station manager for two days and it costs them a fortune."

When you hear a few stories like that you begin to under- stand why courier companies are constantly hoping that someday they'll be able to find a way to avoid using on-boards at all. All the more reason to make a special effort to be on time and follow in- structions to the letter. Dress neatly and don't roll off the plane blind drunk. By conducting yourself in a professional manner at all times, you are not only helping establish your own reputation but you are doing a favor for all freelance on-board couriers.

✈ ✈ ✈ ✈

About the time the first edition Air Courier Bargains was hitting the bookstores, the civilized world went charging into Kuwait and the world of travel went into a tailspin. I learned a very important lesson in the process: Times of trouble are terrific times to travel.

Travel to Europe from the United States and England was way off due to the fear — misplaced, as it turned out — of terrorism. The result was a slew of bargains for fearless travelers. Airlines, eager to recoup lost business, lowered fares; hotels, desperate to fill empty rooms, offered substantial discounts. But if there were savings for everyone, there were super-bargains for couriers. During this period, I noted $99 round-trip courier fares from New York to Geneva, Copenhagen, Amsterdam, and Madrid — even to London and Paris where discounts of any sort tend to be rare.

A similar phenomenon occurred when Mount Pinatubo erupted in the Philippines. One courier company started allowing couriers on its Manila run to take two pieces of checked baggage. The reason: fewer people wanted to visit the Philippines while it was raining ash. The fact that Manila was little affected by the eruption didn't seem to matter.

More recently, incessant media reports about a crime wave against tourists in Mexico City sent courier fares plunging to $50 round-trip at some companies. Couriers who moved on from Mexico City — and that probably means most of them — had nothing to worry about.

✈ ✈ ✈ ✈

The Holy Grail of the avid courier is the free flight. They are available. They are not available every day of the week, but they crop up with surprising regularity. In my case, because I monitor flight availability so regularly, I have found that it's not the free flights that are so rare but the free flights that coincide with my schedule!

Many air courier companies have established procedures for handling last-minute openings. I have given complete details (when available) in the "International Air Courier Directory."

Here is a strategy to use regardless of whether the courier company has published guidelines for last-minute openings. It works best if you have already established a track record as a reliable courier, but I know of first-time couriers who have used it successfully. It requires that you be ready to go at a moment's notice (i.e., you have a bag already packed) and be willing to go to any destination to which the courier company travels.

Give all the courier companies in your preferred departure cities a call and briefly explain your situation. "I'm available to travel to any of your destinations from Monday the fourth to Sunday the tenth. Call me if you get a cancellation. Of course, since I'm willing to go anywhere on such short notice, I'll expect your absolute lowest fare."

If the company has established last-minute fares, they may not be subject to negotiation. Otherwise, you should feel free to negotiate for the lowest fare when you first call or, if you have the gall, when they call you and you know they're desperate. Be careful, however. The courier companies provide you with a very good deal. Taking advantage of them when they're in a bind can backfire. After all, it's a small world.

Another possible ploy is to call with basically the same proposition except that this time you say, "I'm only willing to go if you can waive the fare. So call me only if you're really desperate. I guarantee that I will be able to leave for the airport as soon as you call me."

Either approach presupposes that you will be able to deliver on your promise. If they call and you say, "Oh, gee, well my plans changed and I can't make it," you can forget ever dealing with that company again. It follows that if you book a flight with one company using this strategy, you *immediately* call any others you have contacted and inform them that you have booked a flight and are no longer available.

Don't overlook timing when laying your plans to grab a free or ultra-low cost fare. "During the summer months, getting a free flight is almost impossible," says George Sprague, speaking of the Far Eastern destinations that are his favorites. "All the college kids are out of school and they're willing to pay the regular fare.

But if you go in November, December, January, or February — which is the best time of year to go to places like Singapore and Bangkok — you can almost always get a free flight."

And don't forget other factors that might create a window of opportunity for the die-hard bargain hunter. As I noted earlier, both the Gulf War and the eruption of Mt. Pinatubo spawned a rash of low-cost courier flights for those brave enough to go against conventional wisdom.

At the far end of the spectrum, of course, are those couriers who are available all the time to go anywhere. If you have established yourself with a courier company as someone who *regularly* takes advantage of last-minute flights then it may not be so important that you are not available on one particular occasion. The courier company will simply go on to the next call and keep you on their list.

Remember that there is competition for these low- or no-cost opportunities. Some companies have told me that they have long lists of people who say they are available at short notice. Your challenge is to give yourself every possible advantage.

Even though the courier company may have a "take a number and wait in line" system — or claim they do — a simple understanding of human nature tells us that other factors come into play. For one thing, human beings play favorites, which is why it is so important to establish your profile as a reliable courier. When a slot opens up, you want them to think of you first.

I also suspect that you can better your chances by making it easier for the company to remember you and contact you. For example, if you are telling a company that you are available to travel during the coming week, you might want to fax them a sort of advertisement for your availability that they can stick up on their bulletin board. That way if something comes up, your eye-catching notice may give you an advantage. If you are constantly looking for available flights, consider providing the companies in your area of interest with tabbed Rolodex cards that say something like "Emergency Courier," or "Last-Minute Courier to England.

Even if you follow all of the above advice, it's still a good idea to check in with the courier company every day to find out if something's opened up. I was told by one West Coast courier coordinator that when he needs a last-minute replacement he dutifully goes down the list of people who have said they are "always" available only to hear them say, "Gosh, I can't go tomorrow — but keep me on the list." Invariably, so he told me, he winds up filling the slot with someone who just happened to call up out of the blue and say, "I'd like to go somewhere. What do you have available?" In my own experience, the great deals I've received have been about equally divided between those that simply fell into my lap when a courier company called me up and those that I got because I just happened to call in at the right time with a yen to travel.

✈ ✈ ✈ ✈

The final frontier for the avid courier is finding a way of flying as a courier with companies that will swear up and down that they never use freelance on-board couriers.

"If a company claims it's not using an on-board courier," says Steinberg, "then it cannot be in control of how quickly its packages get across the Atlantic because its packages must be going with the airline as air freight when the airline next sends out a freight plane. Now they're not in control of how long the things stay in the airline's warehouse before they get loaded onto the plane or when the plane is going because there's no such thing as a scheduled air freight service, really. And they're not in control of off-loading the stuff when it gets to wherever it's going. I'd always be very suspicious if people say they don't use on-board couriers anymore."

The fact of the matter is that even the industry heavyweights with their own fleets of planes sometimes need a human being to physically accompany a shipment on a regular airline. The question becomes where do they get them? In some cases, they actually can call on their own people. DHL, for example, has regular runs to the Caribbean that they make available at no cost to their own vacationing employees. Because they are such a large company, they apparently can fill the available slots. When they can't, they turn to a booking agent to plug the holes. It is also possible that a company that normally co-loads with a wholesaler might find itself in a situation in which it temporarily needs to use its own on-board courier.

Sometimes, unusual circumstances can create a need for an on-board courier. "If someone like Salomon Brothers is putting in a bid for a $5 billion company in Europe," muses Steinberg, "and they want someone to hand-carry that bid across, they may contact the courier company they are using at the moment and say 'We've got a special, private, rush job. We want this thing taken over immediately, hand-carried, and hand-delivered. Can you do it?'

"Well, the courier company obviously won't have anyone [on staff] that they can use to do it but they will have a list of people who are reliable who they can use. But the trouble is, it's going to be quite difficult to get on that list, isn't it?"

The "courier curtain" can be difficult, if not impossible, to penetrate. Courier companies, for very good reasons, don't like to discuss their methods of operation with strangers making inquiries on the phone. In any event, it's an assignment only for the die-hard courier who is willing and able to travel at the last minute to anywhere, since that's virtually the only situation in which an opportunity might develop.

If you'd like to try it anyway and you live in or near one of the gateway cities, begin by compiling a list of local courier companies from the phone book. You may be able to eliminate some as being inappropriate, but in this case, it's probably better to canvas them all. Then follow the suggestions given above for last-minute, go-anywhere couriers. Don't bother to phone. Just send a letter to the "Director of Courier Operations" (a good catch-all title) explaining that you are available to travel on short notice as an on-board courier should the need arise. Let them know you are an experienced courier by citing the companies you have flown for and giving references if possible. Then sit back, cross your fingers, and wait for the phone to ring.

Oh yes, one more thing. Don't hold your breath.

✈ ✈ ✈ ✈

If all else fails, you can always hang out a shingle and become a private, freelance courier for companies willing to go to the extra expense of having someone hand carry their precious documents overseas and personally deliver them. That's what Jim Ward (not his real name) has done and so far, he reports, it's working out just fine.

"The business I have received to date has been completely by word of mouth and by contacts built up during my military service," says Jim, who got the itch for the courier's life when he was in the Navy and ferried classified documents to places like Guantanamo, Cuba, and Cadiz, Spain. "I either directly know my client or the person who recommended me. This fact simplifies negotiations as far as I'm concerned. They know my daily fee, pay my expenses, and I try my very best to be on time, remain flexible to schedule changes at either end, and provide them with a detailed report upon completion. Unless I'm on vacation, I don't 'travel the globe' just to see the world. The vast majority of my services has placed me on site at the delivery point on one day and leaving on the next."

Jim's typical client is a high technology company and the typical "cargo" is business-related paperwork. "I read the documents if I can," Jim says by way of explaining how he assures himself he's not getting involved in anything fishy. "At the very least, I know I'm carrying paperwork and nothing but." Jim chooses his flights, usually at full-fare coach, and the client pays for the tickets. They also pay all his expenses such as meals, hotels, and taxis. There is also a per diem fee that varies slightly from client to client and situation to situation but which averages "several hundred dollars" per day. Jim tells me that he makes several trips a month.

When he arrives at his destination, a representative of the company to which the documents are being delivered will meet him at the airport — just like a "regular" courier flight. Less frequently, he will travel to the consignee's offices to drop off the package. After that, it's a matter of relaxing until the return flight. If Jim wants to stay for a few extra days to see the sights, he picks up any extra costs. Most of Jim's private courier jobs have taken him to London or Germany, although a trip to the Czech Republic is in the offing. He also looks forward to work that will take him to the Pacific Rim nations.

The upside of Jim's strategy is that the client pays his way from the very beginning. Not only is his ticket taken care of, he even gets reimbursed for the cost of a taxi to the airport. The downside to following Jim's example is that finding customers — honest, reliable customers, at least — can be a problem. Jim had a leg up in that he retained many contacts from his days in the military who were able to refer him to potential customers. They in turn recommended him to their business acquaintances and colleagues. Building such a clientele from scratch could be a long, arduous, and expensive proposition. Indeed, Jim reports that his efforts at marketing his services outside his circle of regular customers have proven disappointing; it's still very much a referral business.

As exotic as his lifestyle may sound, Jim downplays the glamour. "I'm not James Bond," he says. "I'm just a delivery boy."

Part II

International
Air Courier
Directory

Introduction to the Directory

In the following chapters, I provide listings of courier companies and booking agencies throughout the world. The arrangement is somewhat idiosyncratic, as follows:

Canada: Cities are listed alphabetically which coincidentally means they also are listed in order from east to west.

United States: Here the arrangement is more obviously geographical, starting with the east coast and moving westward — Boston, New York, Washington, DC, Miami, Detroit, Chicago, San Francisco, and Los Angeles.

Europe: The bulk of this chapter is devoted to England. Since most of the courier companies in England are clustered to the west of London, around Heathrow airport, I have arranged them alphabetically by company name.

The Pacific Rim, and Latin America: Each is a separate chapter, with contacts listed alphabetically by country, then by city, then by company name.

Destination Index: This index allows you to link cities with the air courier companies that serve them.

Additional explanatory notes and comments appear at the beginning of each chapter. It may not be the most elegant arrangement, but it strikes me as serviceable.

Most of the companies listed are actively dealing with freelance couriers. However, I have included a few companies (a very few) that used to use freelancers but have discontinued the practice. Why? For the simple reason that policies change — sometimes overnight.

For each contact, I have tried to give a comprehensive overview of their current situation. Don't assume, however, that the entries are encyclopedic. In other words, just because a listing of courier company "x" makes no mention of last-minute, reduced fares doesn't automatically mean they are never offered.

Some Do's and Don'ts

The best way to inquire about flights is to telephone. Don't fax questions about policies or queries about flight availability; you won't get an answer (they don't have time) and will succeed in alienating the courier company. Remember, these people are in the freight business, not the passenger business. You will endear yourself to them by making their job as easy as possible.

If you haven't read the first part of this book, do so before making your first call. You'll be doing everyone a favor, yourself included.

A Final Note

Companies go out of business and new ones spring up to take their place. Companies that use freelance couriers today may change their policy tomorrow. You will always have to double-check to see what the current policy is and what flights are available. The same applies in reverse. Companies not listed here may begin to seek freelancers. If you find any, please let me know.

Drop a postcard to The Intrepid Traveler, P.O. Box 438, New York, NY 10034, or email to courier@intrepidtraveler. com. Finally, in a year or so, go back to the bookstore where you got this book. I'll probably have a new edition out by then!

CANADA

A las, the Canada chapter of this book seems to grow slimmer every edition. I almost considered combining it with the United States chapter but, ever sensitive to the desire of my northern neighbors to stress their apartness from the behemoth to the south, I have retained the current structure.

All fares listed from Canadian cities are quoted in Canadian dollars, which trade at about a 40 percent discount to the American dollar. Factor that in when doing your budgeting.

[*Note:* To dial direct to Canada from the United Kingdom, first dial the international access code (00). Then dial (1), which is Canada's "country code." Then dial the numbers listed below. From the United States, of course, a call to Canada is like any other long-distance call.]

✈ ✈ ✈ ✈

MONTREAL

F.B. On-Board Courier Service
5110 Fairway Street
Lachine, Quebec H8T 1B8
(514) 631-2677 to book flights
(514) 631-7925, administrative offices
(514) 633-0735 (Fax)

At present F.B.'s Montreal operation books couriers to London from Montreal with add-on service offered from Toronto. There had been some talk of a run to Paris, but it has yet to happen. The length of stay varies with the day of departure as follows:

Destination (Airline)	Departure Days	Length of Stay	Fare Range
London (Air Canada)	Monday-Friday	Up to 30 days	$525 – $625

The fare range reflects high and low seasons. The high season is from June 15 through September 15 and from December 15 through the end of the year. In the case of last-minute availabilities, the fare may drop by $100. F.B.'s quoted fares include departure tax. The courier is restricted to carry on luggage only. All flights are on Air Canada and the courier can collect frequent flyer miles.

You must carry a passport that allows you to enter England without a visa. Payment is by cash, cashier's check, or money order. No credit cards are accepted. There is no return guarantee deposit. Call the flight booking number above between 9:00 a.m. and 12:00 noon EST to book flights; ask to speak with Roeland Denooij. After those hours an answering machine picks up and you can leave your name and address to have a descriptive brochure sent. Use the administrative office number only in emergencies.

TORONTO

F.B. On-Board Courier Service
5110 Fairway Street
Lachine, Quebec H8T 1B8
(514) 631-2677 to book flights
(514) 631-7925, administrative offices
(514) 633-0735 (Fax)

F.B. no longer has flights directly to London out of Toronto. However, you can make arrangements through their Montreal office (above) to fly to Montreal to connect with a courier flight from there. Prices are the same as if you were departing from Montreal. All bookings are handled in Montreal.

VANCOUVER

F.B. On-Board Courier Service
4871 Miller Road
Suite 107E
Richmond, British Columbia V7B 1K8
(604) 278-1266
(604) 278-5367 (Fax)

F.B.'s Vancouver operation offers four flights each week to London on Tuesday, Wednesday, Thursday, and Saturday. Recently, round-trip fares were being quoted at $690 including all taxes on both ends; the price, I am told, does not vary during the year.

There is a variable stay of from 7 to 30 days. Flights return from London on Tuesday, Wednesday, Thursday, and Sunday. There is just one courier slot per day from London, so if the day you choose for your return flight is already taken, you'll have to choose again. If there is absolutely no availability, they will double book (i.e. put two couriers on the same return flight), but they tell me this is very rare.

Tickets can be booked three months in advance, but a recent inquiry revealed no openings at all for nearly three months, so it obviously pays to plan ahead for this run. Flights are via Air Canada and offer frequent flyer points. The courier is restricted to carry-on baggage only and functions as a courier in both directions.

Flights to Hong Kong have been discontinued. Expedited freight service on this route can now be accomplished without the use of on-board couriers.

Unlike the Toronto office, the Vancouver office handles its own bookings. Ask for Jim Marshall when you call, although anyone in the office can help you. Payment may be made in cash or by personal check. They do not accept credit cards.

F.B. does maintain a list for last-minute openings in their flight schedule. When a slot opens up they go down the list and the first person available gets the flight. Prices can drop by 50% in these situations. I am told they prefer to deal with people who live in Vancouver. However, if you live in Seattle and can convince them you'll drop everything to dash to Vancouver on short notice, they may add you to the list.

UNITED STATES

This chapter is arranged geographically, from East to West and North to South. That is, you will find courier gateway cities listed in the following order: Boston, New York, Washington, DC, Miami, Detroit, Chicago, San Francisco, and Los Angeles. Courier service from **Houston** to Mexico, London, and Tokyo has been absent for so long, that it is unlikely to return. If it does, it's a good bet that the courier booking agency Now Voyager (see the New York listings) will know about it.

If a company has offices in more than one city, I have given the most complete information about policies and procedures under the office in the "headquarters" city.

[*Note:* to dial direct to the United States from the United Kingdom, first dial (010) which tells the phone company you are making an international call. Then dial (1), which is the United States' "country code." Then dial the numbers listed below. From Canada, of course, a call to the United States is like any other long-distance call.]

✈ ✈ ✈ ✈

BOSTON

Halbart Express
147-05 176th Street
Jamaica, NY 11434
(718) 656-8189
(718) 244-0559 (Fax)
web site: http://www.halbart.com

Halbart is a New York City-based wholesaler and a major player in the air courier business (see the New York listings for more information about their policies and procedures.)

They maintain a Boston office from which they offer occasional courier flights to London. Typically, these flights do not fly directly to London but stop in New York first. When available, these flights cost about the same or slightly more than the then-prevailing fares on the New York-London run, and involve the same luggage and length-of-stay restrictions.

Despite the Boston departure, all bookings must be made through the New York office.

✈ ✈ ✈ ✈

NEW YORK

New York is without a doubt the air courier capital of the United States. No other gateway city comes close, either in terms of the number of companies booking on-board couriers or the number of destinations served.

There are two major booking agencies in the New York area: Air-Tech and Now Voyager. While there is a good bit of overlap in their listings, they don't offer precisely the same flights, and at any given time one may be sitting on a last-minute special that the other doesn't know about, so you may find it worth your while to check with both to see what they are offering at any given time. Another differentiator is the level and quality of service they provide. You, the consumer, will have to be the judge of that.

That's not to say that excellent opportunities can't be found elsewhere — through other, smaller, operations or directly with air freight wholesalers and retailers. They can. The following listings give the details.

Air Cargo Partners (ACP)
(a.k.a. VEX Wholesale Express)
Virgin Atlantic Airlines
149-32 132nd Street
JFK International Airport
Jamaica, NY 11430
(888) VEX-MOVE (839-6683)
(718) 529-6814, ext. 4
(718) 529-6817 (Fax)

This is the in-house courier operation of Virgin Atlantic Cargo. Air Cargo Partners (ACP) is a new name for this operation and many couriers are familiar with it as VEX Wholesale Express.

ACP's sole destination is London. According to station manager, Raj Kundi, Virgin has it eye on other destinations as well, but don't hold your breath. The schedule is as follows:

Destination	Departure Days	Length of Stay	Fare Range
London (from JFK)	Twice daily	Up to 6 weeks	$340-$660
London (from EWR)	Daily	Up to 6 weeks	$430-$510

ACP's operation offers a number of attractions for would-be couriers. Not only are there three flights daily to London (Heathrow), two from New York's JFK and one from Newark

103

International (EWR), but couriers are allowed their full luggage allotment — two bags of up to 70 pounds each. The JFK flights depart at 7:30 p.m. and 10:55 p.m. From Newark, flights leave at 9:25 p.m. These flights will be especially attractive to two people who both want to get to London as couriers on the same day.

The downside is that ACP's fares are considerably higher than those available from Halbart (see below). In fact, consolidator fares and even Virgin Atlantic's own published sales fares are sometimes lower than those offered by its courier operation. All flights go to London's Heathrow airport and fares are cheapest from JFK in the winter and from Newark in the summer. All fares include departure tax.

ACP also operates London runs from Los Angeles (departing at 5:30 p.m.), Washington, DC (6:45 p.m.), and San Francisco (4:30 p.m.). All three are booked by ACP's New York office. There is one flight a day from each of these cities.

Another plus to ACP's London run is that there is no minimum stay, making it an option for a long weekend. While you are free to pick your own return date, you are not guaranteed your first choice. The roster fills up on a first-come, first-served basis. If another courier is already slated to return on that date, ACP will try to get you back either the day before or the day after. If your schedule is carved in stone, you will be wise to book early.

Bookings can be made up to two months in advance and you can pay with a credit card. Cash, certified checks, and money orders are also accepted. ACP will take a personal check if there is sufficient time before the flight. A return-guarantee deposit is not required. Couriers must be at least 18 years of age and fill out an application form. You will have to provide ACP with a photocopy of your passport and any required visas.

ACP has a graduated refund policy if you cancel a booked flight. It works like this: more than 56 days before the flight date, ACP will retain your deposit or 25% of the fare, whichever is higher; from 56 to 30 days, they retain your deposit or 50% whichever is higher; 29 days to one day before the flight, they take 90% of the fare. If you cancel on the day of the flight, you lose the entire fare. They require couriers to check in by telephone one week before flight date to reconfirm their flight; *fail-*

ure to do so can result in the cancellation of your reservation and trigger the cancellation penalties outlined above.

ACP no longer maintains a list of people interested in last-minute travel, although short-notice availabilities do crop up from time to time. The latest ACP books "last-minute" departures is two days prior to the flight; they need that long to complete the paperwork and cut the ticket. If you're interested, give them a call. While the fare will be discounted somewhat, don't expect huge savings.

You can find staff members in the ACP office from 10:00 a.m. to 6:00 p.m. The recorded menu you get when you call lists several companies; press number "four" at any time during this message to be connected directly to ACP's travel department, where Janet or Leslie can take your booking.

Air Facility

153-40 Rockaway Boulevard
Jamaica, NY 11434
(718) 712-1769
(718) 712-2597 (Fax)
email: obc@airfacility.com
web site: http://www.airfacility.com

Air Facility is an air courier wholesaler serving the following South American destinations:

Destination (Airline)	Departure Days	Length of Stay	Typical Fare
Buenos Aires (UA)	Monday	9 days	$480
	Tuesday	7 days	
	Wednesday	15 days	
	Thursday	8 days	
	Saturday	9 days	
Caracas (UA)	Tuesday	9 days	$210
	Wednesday	7 days	
	Thursday	8 days	
	Saturday	14 days	

Destination (Airline)	Departure Days	Length of Stay	Typical Fare
Mexico City (Aeromexico)	Monday	9 days	$180
	Tuesday	7 days	
	Wednesday	8 days	
	Thursday	4 days	
	Saturday	6 days	
Montevideo (UA)	Monday	9 days	$480
	Tuesday	7 days	
	Wednesday	15 days	
	Thursday	8 days	
	Saturday	9 days	
Rio (Varig)	Monday	10 days	$480
	Tuesday	7 days	
	Wednesday	14 days	
	Thursday	8 days	
	Sunday	8 days	
Sao Paulo (Varig)	Monday – Thursday, Saturday	8 - 13 days	$480

Notes: The length of stay varies with the day of departure. Call to confirm the current schedule. The run to Brazil requires a tourist visa for U.S. citizens; obtaining the visa is the courier's responsibility. Only one carry-on bag is allowed on all of Air Facility's flights.

Be aware that fares rise sharply during the last two weeks of December when many people travel for the holidays. To Buenos Aires, Montevideo, Rio, and Sao Paulo, the fare rises to between $550 and $650; to Caracas it is $300 and up, and to Mexico City it is in the $250 to $300 range. Perhaps to compensate for the higher fares, Air Facility offers longer stays during this holiday period. Service to Madrid and Santiago has been discontinued.

Office hours are 9:00 a.m. to 4:30 p.m. EST, Monday to Friday. The On-Board Courier Specialist handling all booking matters is Marisa Marsico.

Air Facility requires that its couriers be at least 18 years of age; there is no upper age cutoff. You must be either a citizen of the U.S. or have resident alien status (that is, you must possess a "green card"). Non-residents who are in the U.S. on tourist visas can sometimes fly with Air Facility if they have a sufficient amount of time left on their visas. This is decided on a case by case basis.

You can book up to two months in advance, and they prefer it if you book at least one month in advance, and then pay within seven days of making the reservation by cash, certified check, or money order; no credit cards or personal checks are accepted. You can cancel your reservation and get a refund up to 14 days before the flight.

If you are available to fly at short notice, call and let them know the dates you are available and the destination(s) you are willing to accept. If they get a cancellation, they may give you a call. However, I am told they maintain a list of "most likely" couriers for last-minute availabilities. Typically, they will sell these last-minute openings for about $100 off list price and refund whatever they realize on the ticket to the person who was forced to cancel.

Airhitch

2641 Broadway, Suite 100
New York, NY 10025
(800) 326-2009
(212) 864-2000
email: airhitch@netcom.com
web site: http://www.airhitch.org

Airhitch is not an air courier company, but a student-run organization specializing in space-available travel to Europe at steep discounts comparable to those available to couriers. Here's how it works:

Register with Airhitch, giving them the earliest, latest, and preferred dates of departure, the "region" from which you wish to depart, and three choices of destination in Europe. You are instructed to call back as your "date-range" approaches; they will tell you what's available. You must accept one of the flights offered — even if it's not from your ideal departure point or to your primary destination — or forfeit your fare. Like air courier operations, Airhitch is designed for the independent traveler for whom a change in destination will be an adventure, not a disaster.

Airhitch lists its "primary" destinations as Amsterdam, Athens, Barcelona, Dusseldorf, Frankfurt, London, Lisbon, Luxembourg, Madrid, Milan, Paris, Rome, and Shannon. But cities can be added and scratched from the list at dizzying speed. Current one-way fares are $159 from New York, $189 from the southeast, $239 from the west coast, and $209 from the midwest, "when available." Return trips are booked separately, through an Airhitch associate in Europe. Of course, you can elect to use Airhitch in only one direction. There is also a "Target Flight" program that will provide you with a confirmed seat from a specific place to a specific place on a specific date — at a higher price, of course.

For those who don't live in or near the major jumping-off points for couriers, Airhitch's best feature may be the range of departure cities it offers. European flights have been available (on an irregular basis) from Seattle, Denver, Minneapolis, Detroit, Tampa, Fort Lauderdale, Baltimore, and Cleveland.

Airhitch claims that 90% of their travelers flew directly to one of their preferred destinations or to a city within "commuting distance," and that 100% of registrants "who followed our guidelines" flew during their "date-range." The Airhitch system favors those who register far in advance of their desired travel dates, as the date of registration determines the order in which people are offered available seats. It also helps if you can spend an extended amount of time in Europe.

A similar "Sunhitch" service offers the Caribbean during the winter months. Here the registration fee is $199 from the east coast, $229 from the midwest, $209 from the west coast to Pacific coast destinations in Mexico, and $249 from the west coast to the Caribbean region. All registrations are for a round trip and a one-week stay. You must specify a five-day date range and be willing to accept any resort destination, which could mean Puerta Vallarta, St. Maarten, or half a dozen destinations in between. Most of these trips provide a confirmed return exactly seven days after departure, but some trips require you to stand by on the return as well.

Airhitch also sells domestic airlines ("Domestic Airhitch") on the same space-available basis. Currently they offer transcontinental flights (from the Northeast or Florida to the West Coast) for $119, the west coast to Hawaii for the same price, the Northeast to Florida for $79, and the Midwest to either coast also for $79. All fares are one-way. You have to make yourself available to leave within a three-day range.

Airhitch has a brochure with detailed information on their policies and procedures. The New York office is open 10:00 a.m. to 5:00 p.m. EST. After hours, a voice mail system — the "Airhitch Robot" — provides extensive information about their offerings. There are also offices in Los Angeles and San Francisco.

Unfortunately, there's a downside to all this. You should be aware that, from time to time, Airhitch has been known to strand passengers in Europe. In these cases, the hapless travelers wind up having to shell out a considerable amount of money to pay their own way back. From what I have been able to gather, disasters like this are the exception rather than the rule. But that will be scant comfort should you find yourself stuck at the airport with no way home. I have been told by people unlucky enough to have suffered this fate that Airhitch has not been very forthcoming in responding to their complaints, much less reimbursing them for their out-of-pocket expenses in getting home.

You can reduce the odds of becoming stranded by avoiding times of peak travel. August and early September is one such period, when thousands of vacationers are thronging the airports to return home. The downside risk may scare you off Airhitch. On the other hand, you may feel the odds are in your favor and decide to take a chance. If so you can register by phone or on Airhitch's extensive web site, which also explains the Airhitch system in great detail.

Air-Tech Ltd.
588 Broadway
Suite 204
New York, NY 10012
(212) 219-7000, ext. 206
(212) 219-0066 (Fax)
email: fly@airtech.com
web site: http://www.airtech.com

"Europe Sucks! Why spend more than $169 getting there?" That's the headline on an Air-Tech flyer and it pretty much captures the spirit of this hip, young operation that operates out of a busy office in the historic Soho district.

Air-Tech has its fingers in a number of budget travel pies. Of immediate interest is the fact that they offer yet another source of courier bookings in the New York area. At press time, Air-Tech was offering courier flights to the following destinations:

Destination (Airline)	Departure Days	Length of Stay	Fare Range
Amsterdam (UA)	Call	7 days	$250–$400
Auckland	Very iffy	Up to 30 days	$1000
Bangkok (UA)	Call	1 week to 3 months	$500–$700
Beijing (UA)	Call	1 week to 3 months	$650–$800
Brisbane (Qantas)	Call	1 week to 3 months	$1000–$1200
Brussels (UA)	Daily except Friday	7 days	$250–$400

Destination (Airline)	Departure Days	Length of Stay	Fare Range
Buenos Aires (LanChile, UA)	Call	Up to 2 weeks	$550
Cairns (Qantas)	Call	1 week to 3 months	$1000-$1200
Caracas (UA)	Call	Up to 2 weeks	$200-$400
Copenhagen (KLM, AA)	Call	1 week	$200-$400
Dublin (Aer Lingus)	Call	1 week	$250-$400
Hong Kong (UA, JAL)	Call	1 week to 3 months	$300-$650
Johannesburg (SAA)	Call	Up to 45 days	$900-$1000
London (AA, UA)	Call	1 week to 1 month	$275-$400
Manila (UA)	Call	1 week to 3 months	$600-$800
Melbourne (Qantas)	Call	1 week to 3 months	$1000-$1200
Milan (TWA)	Call	1 week to 2 weeks	$250-$450

Destination (Airline)	Departure Days	Length of Stay	Fare Range
Montevideo (Varig)	Call	Up to 2 weeks	$550
Paris (TWA)	Daily except Friday	7 days	$350-$450
Rio de Janeiro (Varig)	Call	Up to 2 weeks	$350-$550
Rome (TWA)	Call	1 week to 2 weeks	$250-$450
Sao Paulo (Varig)	Call	Up to 2 weeks	$350-$550
Seoul (UA)	Call	1 week to 3 months	$700-$800
Shanghai (UA)	Call	1 week to 3 months	$650-$800
Singapore (JAL)	Call	1 week to 3 months	$500-$600
Sydney (Qantas)	Call	1 week to 3 months	$1000-$1200
Taipei (UA)	Call	1 week to 3 months	$650-$800
Tokyo (UA)	Call	1 week to 3 months	$500-$700

Flights to Brisbane, Cairns, Melbourne, and Sydney are actually one flight. That is there is one flight a day to Australia and the courier can terminate at any of these cities on a first-come, first-served basis. Flights to Rome and Milan involve different lengths of stay depending on the day of departure; call for specific information.

Most routes restrict the courier to carry-on baggage only. However, some routes let the courier return with one checked bag, so be sure to ask which restrictions apply to your trip.

It's best to book two months in advance, although Air-Tech occasionally has last-minute specials to offer. Among the bargain fares available recently were $100 to London and $350 to Rio. There have even been free flights to Copenhagen and Singapore. Air-Tech accepts personal checks more than two weeks before flight date. Otherwise it's cash, certified checks, and money orders. They also accept Visa, MasterCard, and Discover credit cards. Return-guarantee deposits are required on some of these flights. Air-Tech also books courier flights out of Los Angeles, but only from its New York office. See the LA section (below) for more information.

Courier flights are a sideline for Air-Tech. Their major focus is space available air travel on the Airhitch model, although they claim to have solved the stranding problems that have angered some Airhitch customers. According to Air-Tech President, Mike Esterson, the best way to avoid problems is to avoid peak travel periods. "The last week of July through the first two weeks of August is the worst time to try to come back from Europe," he notes. "We try to steer people away from dates we know are going to be heavily booked." Air-Tech also says they will work with European travel agents (primarily in Paris) to find their customers cheap return alternatives.

Air-Tech also claims to have especially good working relationships with the airlines they book on. Esterson says that many of their customers leave for Europe with return standby tickets (as opposed to a voucher) on the airline they fly over on. It doesn't guarantee a seat, but it adds an extra layer of probability. Still, the nature of "space available" is that sometimes space simply isn't — available, that is. Bear that in mind before taking your chances.

Otherwise, the procedures are much the same as with

Airhitch. One-way fares to Europe are $169 (plus $10 tax) from the East Coast, $199 (plus tax) from the Midwest, and $229 (plus tax) from the West Coast. "Potential" destinations during the high season listed as Amsterdam, Brussels, London, Manchester, Luxemburg, Frankfurt, Dusseldorf, Madrid, Paris, Milan, Rome, Ireland, and Greece. In the off season, the list shrinks somewhat. Once in Europe, the traveler must contact Air-Tech's Paris agent to arrange the return flight. See the Europe section (below) for more information.

Air-Tech also runs a space available service to major Mexican resorts and several Caribbean islands, including Jamaica, St. Lucia, and the Bahamas. They try to get you to the destination you want within the two- or three- day window you agree on. The way the game is played, however, means that you may request Jamaica and be offered Cancun. However, they offer flights from Washington, Baltimore, Philadelphia, New York, Boston, Chicago, Denver, San Francisco, and Los Angeles, so if you can be flexible about where you leave from, they say, you can probably get where you want to go when you want to go there. Once you get your ticket, however, you will have a confirmed return, generally seven days later, but sometimes sooner. The good news is that the round-trip fare is just $199 to $250 for a seven-day stay. If you are willing to accept standby status for the return leg, you can stay longer, but expect to be charged a standby "penalty" in the $20 range when you board the return flight. Using a similar arrangement, they offer $129 one-way flights to Hawaii from the West Coast.

Air-Tech has branched out into selling consolidator and other discount tickets. In some cases they operate as true consolidators, that is, they have contracts directly with some airlines. In other cases, they function as brokers. Their major areas of specialty are Europe and Asia. Expect a discount of between 20% and 30% off "regular" fares.

Air-Tech maintains branch offices in Boston, Philadelphia, Baltimore, and Washington, DC, most of them operated in conjunction with Hostelling International. At these offices you can purchase Air-Tech space-available vouchers or get information on courier flights.

To reach the courier department quickly, dial (212) 219-7000 and press extension 206 as soon as you hear the recorded message. After regular business hours, the recorded message at that extension carries information on last-minute specials, if any are currently available. The courier contacts are Greg Latkin and Rita Parr.

Be aware that no New York booking agency's listings precisely match those of the others. To get the fullest selection, you will have to check with all of them.

All Nations Express
149-35 177th Street
Room 103
Jamaica, NY 11434
(718) 553-1718
(718) 553-1720 (Fax)

"All Nations" may be overstating things a bit, but this small courier company can get you to Seoul, Korea, for somewhere between $650 and $800 round-trip. The higher fares are for summer travel. Flights are on Asiana and leave Monday through Thursday and Saturday.

Mr. Lee Chang Yeoul (who attended middle school across the street from my old Army base in Taegu!) is your friendly guide here. Bookings can be made over the phone. Visa and MasterCard are accepted, as are personal checks; payment must be made at least 10 days prior to flight time.

A glance at their booking sheet for one month revealed that all the passengers were Koreans, which may explain why All Nations seldom has last-minute openings. When they do, says Mr. Lee, the price does not go down.

Brink's Air Courier
1 Battery Park Plaza
New York, NY 10004
(212) 635-3420

No freelancers. Brinks uses its own highly trained and bonded specialists to transport extremely valuable cargo, such as diamonds, to the far corners of the globe. I have listed them here specifically because Brink's is a great company to work for and an excellent career choice if you want a job that includes international travel. If you're interested, send a resume to Human Resources, at the above address.

Courier Network
(Israpak Courier)
515 West 29th Street
New York, NY 10001
(212) 947-3738

Courier Network flies from New York to Tel Aviv six days a week, from Monday through Saturday, and uses freelancers. It's obviously a very popular route. A recent inquiry turned up a cancellation in nine weeks; the next regularly scheduled flight available was more than three months away. Stays in Israel can range from two weeks to two months. The flight out to Israel takes a day and a half, the return trip, one day. Keep that in mind when planning your length of stay. "Most people go for at least two weeks," they tell me.

Another attraction is that you will be allowed one checked piece of luggage in addition to your carry-on allotment. The round-trip fare varies from $500 to $700 depending on the time of year and the fare deal they've been able to negotiate with the airline.

Many of Courier Network's couriers plan their vacations in Israel, I am told. Consequently, they say, there is little call for last-minute couriers. Nonetheless, they will take your name, just in case, if you are free to travel on short notice. To inquire about flight availability and to book your trip, call between 6:30 p.m. and 8:30 p.m. EST. Ask for Yossi.

East-West Express
149-35 177th Street
Jamaica, NY 11434
(718) 656-6246
(718) 656-6247 (Fax)

East-West books couriers from both New York and Los Angeles, but all bookings are made from their New York office.

At press time, they were offering the following destinations:

Destination (Airline)	Departure Days	Length of Stay	Fare Range
Auckland (Qantas)	Saturday	Up to 30 days	$100–$1300
Bangkok (NW)	Tuesday – Saturday	Up to 90 days	$600–$800
Beijing (NW)	Tues, Wed, Saturday	Up to 90 days	$600–$800
Brisbane (Qantas)	Tuesday– Saturday	Up to 90 days	$1000–$1400
Cairns (Qantas)	Tuesday– Saturday	Up to 90 days	$1000–$1400
Capetown (SAA)	Tuesday– Saturday	Up to 60 days	$900–$1200
Hong Kong (NW)	Tuesday – Saturday	Up to 90 days	$600–$800
Johannesburg (SAA)	Tuesday – Saturday	Up to 60 days	$900–$1200
Manila (NW)	Tuesday – Saturday	Up to 90 days	$600–$800
Melbourne (Qantas)	Tuesday– Saturday	Up to 90 days	$1000–$1400
Seoul (NW)	Tuesday – Saturday	Up to 90 days	$600–$800

Destination (Airline)	Departure Days	Length of Stay	Fare Range
Shanghai (NW)	Wednesday	Up to 90 days	$600–800
Singapore (NW)	Tuesday – Saturday	Up to 90 days	$600–$800
Sydney (Qantas)	Tuesday – Saturday	Up to 90 days	$1000–$1400
Taipei (NW)	Tuesday – Saturday	Up to 90 days	$600–$800
Tokyo (NW)	Tuesday – Saturday	Up to 90 days	$600–$800

The Australia run is a single flight which allows the courier to choose Sydney, Melbourne, Brisbane, or Cairns. It makes a stop in Los Angeles, and the courier can originate there. It's booked on a first-come, first-served basis, so if an LA courier books a flight on a given day, that day's run is not available to a courier in New York, and vice versa. None of East-West's Asian destinations has stopovers, but all make connecting flights in Tokyo. Frequent flyer miles are available on Qantas flights but not on Northwest. The run to Johannesburg is on South African Airways; if you are interested in building frequent flyer mileage with them, inquire at the time of booking.

All flights restrict the courier to carry-on luggage only on the outbound leg. Runs to Australia and South Africa allow the courier to check one bag on the return trip. New York couriers meet an East-West representative at JFK airport the night of departure.

To book, you can call up to two months in advance. Tracy Arato, the courier booking agent, generally doesn't open the book earlier than that. Once you have booked, payment must be made within five business days of booking. They accept cash, cashier's checks, or money orders. No credit cards. Personal checks are acceptable if sent well in advance of the departure date. East-West doesn't require a return-guarantee deposit for any of their flights.

If you can travel on short notice, East-West will put you on a list and call you if they have a cancellation, which happens rarely, according to Tracy. The fare in these cases is lower but not exceptionally so. "We've gone down to $400. And if we're really desperate, we'll go even lower, but we're usually not that desperate." Unfortunately, East-West has had little luck with short-notice couriers — no one seems to be available when called on. Needless to say, this provides yet another opening for the reliably flexible courier.

Halbart Express
147-05 176th Street
Jamaica, NY 11434
(718) 656-5000
(718) 244-0559 (Fax)
web site: http://www.halbart.com

Halbart Express serves destinations in Western Europe, the Far East, and occasionally in South America. According to owner Rudy Halbart, they are the largest courier operation in the New York area. All told, Halbart's Director of Development, Jack Schaper, tells me, they fly between six and ten thousand courier flights a year. Halbart is strictly a wholesaler. That is, they ship cargo for other companies that ship it for customers like you and me. Some of the major courier companies such as DHL, Federal Express, Airborne, UPS, and others are Halbart customers.

Recently, the following worldwide destinations were being offered out of New York:

Destination (Airline)	Departure Days	Length of Stay	Fare Range
Amsterdam (KLM/NW)	Monday – Thursday, Saturday	7 days	$278-$478

119

Destination (Airline)	Departure Days	Length of Stay	Fare Range
Bangkok (NW)	Wednesday, Saturday	7–90days	$528-$728
Brussels (KLM/NW)	Monday-Thursday, Saturday	7 days	$278-$478
Copenhagen (KLM/NW)	Monday – Thursday, Saturday	7 days	$278-$478
Dublin (Aer Lingus)	Mon – Thurs Thursday	8 days 7 days	$278-$478
Hong Kong (NW)	Tuesday – Thursday, Saturday	7-90 days	$528-$728
London (AA)	Monday – Saturday	7 days	$228-$378
Madrid (Iberia)	Monday – Thursday, Saturday	8 days 9 days	$378-$678
Manila (NW)	Tuesday – Thursday, Saturday	7-21 days	$428-$628
Milan (TWA)	Monday Tue-Wed-Thurs Saturday	11 days 14 days 7 days	$328-$728

Destination (Airline)	Departure Days	Length of Stay	Fare Range
Paris (TWA)	Monday – Thursday, Saturday	7 days	$328-$528
Rome (TWA)	Monday – Thursday, Saturday	8 days 14 days	$328-$728
Singapore (UA)	Tuesday – Saturday,	7-14 days	$278-$478
Tokyo (Asiana, NW)	Tuesday – Thursday, Saturday	7-28 days	$428-$528

Flights to Tel Aviv and Taipei are no longer available. The run to Sydney is now available only from Halbart's LA office (see the Los Angeles listings).

The fares quoted above include $28 departure tax. Sometimes it may be possible to get shorter or longer stays at some European destinations; ask when you call for information. Flights are also available from Miami (see Miami listings) and Los Angeles (see Los Angeles listings), as well as Chicago (see Chicago listings). There are also occasional flights to London from Boston and Chicago.

Make special note of the lengths of stay in the above table. For example, to Rome, you will have a fixed stay of 8 days if you leave Monday through Thursday; however, you will have a fixed stay of 14 days if you leave on Saturday. On the other hand, courier runs to most Far Eastern destinations feature a flexible stay of from 7 to 21, 28, or 90 days. That means that, subject to availability, you can pick your own date of return within that window.

Policies and Procedures

You can reserve flights over the phone. Once your reservation is made, you must make full payment within three to five business days. You must also provide a photocopy of your passport. You will have to overnight your payment if the flight is less than 14 days away. Payment may be by certified check or money order. No credit cards are accepted. When Halbart receives your payment, they will then send you a contract, which you must sign and return. Only then is your flight secured. At this point, your trip is non-changeable and non-refundable. Expect to post a return-guarantee deposit of $100 by check on the day of departure.

Halbart requires that its couriers be at least 18 years of age and prefer couriers with a U.S. passport. Foreign passports are okay, but Halbart wants to make sure that if you need a visa for your intended destination that you actually have one. They will not book you until they are assured on this point.

Frequent flyer credit is no longer available on American Airlines or Northwest flights. Flight information is available from 9:00 a.m. to 3:00 p.m. EST, Monday through Friday. Ask for Stephanie Sinaly in courier reservations. After hours, you can leave a message for the courier department.

While they use booking agents to find couriers for them, you can also book flights directly. Generally, you can expect to book your flight three to six weeks in advance, although flights are sometimes available on shorter notice. Halbart has a special deal for the last-minute traveler. Call and leave your name and number and the dates you are available to fly. They will call you if there is a last-minute opening. You must be willing to accept whichever destination opens up.

Halbart will refer out-of-town couriers to their travel agency for assistance with connecting flights to JFK. Their web site is of interest primarily to their shipping customers.

Israpak Courier (see Courier Network, above)

Johnny Air Cargo
69-04 Roosevelt Avenue
Woodside, NY 11377
(718) 397-5099
(718) 478-4033 (Fax)

Johnny offers regular courier flights to Manila as follows:

Destination (Airline)	Departure Days	Length of Stay	Fare Range
Manila (Various)	Daily	10 days – 2 months	$299-$899

Johnny uses a variety of airlines on this run including Northwest, Asiana, Korean Airlines, and China Airlines. The courier gets to keep any frequent flyer miles. Couriers must be at least 18 and no older than 55 and are restricted to carry-on luggage in both directions.

Bookings are best made at least two months in advance, although, for busy periods like December, Johnny will take bookings four or more months in advance. Payments can be made by credit card (Visa, MasterCard, American Express), cash, check, or money order. Ask to speak with Sam (she's a lady) or Angel when you're ready to book.

Johnny Air Cargo also offers courier flights to Manila from the west coast. See the listings for Los Angeles and San Francisco for more information on those flights.

Jupiter Air, Ltd.
(MICOM America, Inc.)
Building #14
JFK International Airport
Jamaica, NY 11430
(718) 656-6050
(718) 656-7263 (Fax)
email: juajfk@cris.com

Jupiter Air has four U.S. locations, New York, Chicago, San Francisco, and Los Angeles. Out of New York, they have been offering the following destinations:

Destination (Airline)	Departure Days	Length of Stay	Fare Range
Hong Kong (JAL)	Tuesday – Saturday	7–30 days	$500–$550
Hong Kong (UA)	Daily	7–30 days	$550–$600
London (UA)	Monday – Saturday	7–30 days	$385–$450
Singapore (JAL)	Sunday	7–30 days	$500–$600

All of Jupiter's runs are strictly carry-on only, unless you are staying more than three weeks, in which case you are allowed one checked piece of luggage. For shorter stays you can always pay the excess baggage fee to check a bag if you must. The Hong Kong flight on JAL requires an overnight stay in Tokyo on the return leg, but Jupiter picks up the hotel tab at the lovely Nikko Narita Hotel, including a meal voucher. Once you see the prices on the menus in the hotel restaurants, you'll be glad you have it! If you're going to Singapore, you will have to return on a Wednesday. You can also courier one-way to Hong Kong, London, and Singapore. The one-way fare is one half the current round-trip fare.

Jupiter provides its couriers with extremely detailed instructions, including maps of the customs area at the airport you'll be flying into. Frequent flyer miles are not given on Jupiter flights and it's not much use asking for them. Every courier ticket is stamped "NO AIRLINES MILEAGE."

Flights can be booked six weeks in advance right over the phone. Once you have booked a flight, you must provide payment in full within fourteen days or the booking will automatically be canceled. Bookings are handled by Ron Bracey and

Dania Perez. Payment must be by money order or certified check only. First-time couriers pay a $35 "initiation fee," good for five years, that is valid for travel from any of Jupiter's U.S. locations. All couriers must provide a $100 return-guarantee deposit. In my experience, a check for the deposit is mailed very promptly after your return; you don't even have to ask for it. In addition, Jupiter is now collecting a $7 airport tax.

In Hong Kong, you can deal directly with the Jupiter office there for courier flights to other Asian destinations. I've even booked with the Hong Kong office from the United States, but this means long distance phone calls, faxes, and the cost of obtaining an international bank draft payable in Hong Kong dollars. Obviously, if you took any courier flights from Hong Kong, you'd have to arrange to return to Hong Kong in time to fulfill your obligation as a courier on the Jupiter flight back to the United States. See the Pacific Rim chapter for details.

If you're available to travel at the last minute, ask to be put on Jupiter's emergency waiting list. If a cancellation occurs, you may be offered a fare as low as $250 round-trip. That's the official line, however. Privately, I'm told that when they have a last-minute cancellation, the administrative fee is waived altogether for whoever steps in to make the flight.

Some of the paperwork you receive from Jupiter may bear the business name, MICOM America. Jupiter Air is headquartered in Hong Kong and is a subsidiary of Japan Air. MICOM America is their U.S. franchisee. The contract they have you fill out, however, says Jupiter Air. I list them in this book as Jupiter because that's how all couriers know them.

Now Voyager
74 Varick Street
Suite 307
New York, NY 10013
(212) 431-1616
(212) 334-5243, 219-1753 (Fax)
web site: http://www.nowvoyagertravel.com

Founded in 1984, Now Voyager is the oldest New York booking agency. Like other booking agents, Now Voyager serves a number of different courier companies, thus combining the advantages of one-stop shopping and a wide selection.

Now Voyager charges a $50 annual registration fee. They justify this by pointing out that they mark up their fares less than do other booking agencies. "When we were offering flights to the Caribbean, we were selling them for $50," points out Now Voyager owner, Julie Weinberg. "The other booking agents were charging $99 for these flights — when they could get them. So if it was your first flight, you were paying the same fare. But if it was your second flight with us, you were saving $50." Indeed, the registration fee becomes less of an issue the more frequently you fly.

Destination (Airline)	Departure Days	Length of Stay	Fare Range
Amsterdam (KLM)	Call	7 days	$299-$459
Bangkok (NW, JAL, UA)	Tuesday – Saturday	Up to 3 months	$586-$899
Beijing (NW, JAL, UA)	Tuesday – Saturday	Up to 3 months	$699-$899
Brussels (KLM)	Monday – Saturday	7-30 days	$299-$459
Buenos Aires (Ladeco)	Monday – Thursday, Saturday	9-15 days	$499
Capetown (SAA)	Wednesday	Up to 45 days	$1199-$1299
Caracas (UA)	Tuesday– Thursday, Saturday	8-14 days	$230

Destination (Airline)	Departure Days	Length of Stay	Fare Range
Copenhagen (KLM)	Monday – Thursday, Saturday	7 days	$199-$439
Dublin (Aer Lingus)	Mon–Thurs, Saturday	7-8 days	$299-$459
Frankfurt (TWA)	Mon–Thurs, Saturday	Up to 30 days	$259-$359
Hong Kong (NW, JAL, UA)	Tuesday – Saturday	7 days to 3 months	$438-$899
Johannesburg (SAA)	Wednesday, Friday, Saturday	Up to 45 days	$1029-$1199
London (AA, UA)	Daily	7 days (AA) Up to 30 days (UA)	$199-$399
Madrid (Iberia, TWA)	Monday – Thursday, Saturday	7-15 days	$199-$499
Manila (NW)	Tuesday – Saturday	Up to 3 months	$588-$899
Melbourne (Qantas)	Wednesday, Saturday	Up to 45 days	$699-$1199
Mexico City (Delta)	Daily	3-30 days	$199

Destination (Airline)	Departure Days	Length of Stay	Fare Range
Milan (TWA)	Tuesday – Thursday, Saturday	7–14 days	$250–$550
New Delhi (BA)	Saturday	Up to 120 days	$799
Paris (TWA)	Monday – Thursday	7 days	$259–$439
Rio (Varig)	Mon-Thurs Saturday	7–14 days	$359–$465
Rome (TWA)	Tuesday – Saturday	8–14 days	$250–$550
Sao Paulo (Varig)	Monday – Thursday, Saturday	8–13 days	$359–$455
Seoul (NW, JAL, UA)	Call	7 days – 3 months	$588–$899
Singapore (NW, JAL, UA)	Tuesday – Saturday	7 days – 3 months	$338–$899
Sydney (Qantas, NZ)	Wednesday, Saturday	Up to 45 days	$699–$1199
Taipei (NW, JAL, UA)	Tuesday- Saturday	7 days – 3 months	$559–$899
Tokyo (NW, JAL, UA)	Tuesday – Saturday	7 days – 3 months	$559–$799

Notes: Flights to Santiago and Tel Aviv are no longer offered. To some destinations, such as Rio and Rome, the length of stay will depend on the day of departure; call for details. The New Delhi run has been on-again, off-again, as has been the run to Amsterdam.

The fares quoted are the generally available fares, which fluctuate with the seasons and other supply and demand factors. Flights to Asia vary greatly from month to month. Please be aware that, as with so much in the courier business, these destinations and fares are subject to change. Stockholm and other European destinations have dropped off the list in recent years. Not all destinations listed will be available at any given time. It is best to call their automated attendant (described below) to check on the latest availability.

Non-courier flights

Now Voyager continues to offer special non-courier flights to selected international destinations like Paris, Amsterdam, and Frankfurt (recently for $472 to $493 with a ticket that allows you to fly into one city and return from another). They were also offering flights to Tel Aviv and Cairo on a major US carrier for 25 percent off the regular fare.

Through their wholly owned subsidiary, Mr. Cheap's, Now Voyager also can get you discounted tickets on "eight minor to major airlines." The savings range from 10% to 35% off. Contractual agreements prevent Mr. Cheap's or Now Voyager from revealing the names of the airlines involved and I am not about to reveal them here. Suffice it to say that the airlines are perfectly reputable. The airlines they broker for serve a great many cities and Mr. Cheap's can sell you a ticket from any of them. The result is that Now Voyager is now selling twice as many non-courier flights as they do courier!

Some of these mystery airlines also have destinations in Europe, the Middle East, and the Caribbean. There are also consolidator tickets available for European destinations, as noted above. Non-courier fares to Europe tend to be competitive with courier fares, especially since you can stay for up to three months.

Getting Flight Information from Now Voyager

One of the best things about Now Voyager is that they have an unusually complete "automated attendant" on their line, which means that you have access to recorded information about flight availability, fares, and Now Voyager policies and procedures 24 hours a day. "We update our recording on specials on a regular basis," says owner Weinberg. "We will occasionally get calls from courier companies saying, 'We just lost our courier; can you put the flight on your tape?'"

You can also bypass the automated attendant and get a human being during business hours (which are from 10:00 a.m. to 5:30 p.m. EST, Monday through Friday, and Saturdays from 12:00 to 4:30 p.m.) by pressing "0" at any time.

Here is a tip on using the recorded information line: Tape record it! I have found it impossible to write down all the information they give you — they simply talk too fast.

You can buy a simple, inexpensive hookup from Radio Shack or some similar electronics supply store that lets you record off your phone. Once you've recorded the message, you can replay it and stop it from time to time to allow you to transcribe the information. And don't worry, it's perfectly legal.

Be aware that on any given day it is unlikely that their recording will contain all the destinations listed above. That does not necessarily mean that the destination has been discontinued (although it might). More likely, it means that there are no flights available as of the day of your call. Also, the recording lists "next" available flights, not "all" available flights. If you are booking well in advance (one, two months or more) for a specific destination, you might find it easier to speak with a Now Voyager representative and nail down a departure date.

If you want to book a flight, especially a last-minute flight, your best option may be to simply show up at Now Voyager's doorstep, cash in hand. Some couriers have told me that reaching a live representative on the phone can be a long, frustrating process (although I seem to have pretty good luck). But since no courier booking is absolutely guaranteed until paid for, being there in person can give you an advantage.

It's also possible to show up, bag packed, without a reservation, in the hope that something will turn up during the day. The Now Voyager office is located near Canal Street on Varick; take the 1, 9, A, C, or E subway to Canal Street. Even if you have plenty of time before your intended flight date, always bring your passport when you visit the office.

Policies and Procedures

As noted above, the Now Voyager recording provides you with information on their policies and procedures. Here are some relevant quotes from that recording:

"We book as much as two months in advance. For every destination, we generally book one person per flight. If you are booking for more than one person, they will probably have to fly on consecutive days.

"To book a flight, you must have a valid passport and know where and when you wish to travel. You then give your name and two telephone numbers to your representative and your flight will then be held, in your name, usually for no longer than 24 hours ... We accept cash, money orders, certified checks, and travelers' checks as well as MasterCard, Visa, Diners, Carte Blanche, and American Express. It is slightly less expensive to use cash or traveler's checks. We do not accept personal checks.

"A non-refundable registration fee of $50 is required for the first-time courier and is good for one year."

By "slightly less expensive to use cash or traveler's checks," they mean that they will add three percent to the cost of your flight to cover the fees charged by the credit card companies. All non-cash payments requiring processing time now trigger the three percent additional charge.

In addition, most flights require a $100 return guarantee deposit in the form of a personal check, which will be destroyed upon your return. Most European fares include the $28 departure tax levied at JFK airport.

Most importantly, all flights are non-refundable once paid for. This represents a change from previous policy, which allowed for some refunds if you canceled early enough. Don't make the mistake of giving your credit card number to "hold" your flight while you think it over. Once they take your credit card number,

Now Voyager assumes you have "paid" for the flight and the amount is non-refundable. I suppose you could argue the point with your credit card company, but it's probably better all around to avoid getting into that situation.

Since Now Voyager books for a number of different courier companies, company-specific policies will vary from flight to flight. For example, you may be allowed one checked bag on some runs; on some, you will be a courier in both directions, while on others you will be coming back empty. Usually, the Now Voyager representative will go over the specifics with you, but if they forget, as a reader of this book, you will know the right questions to ask.

Like other courier companies and booking agents, Now Voyager discounts fares as the flight date approaches. They once offered a last-minute trip to Hong Kong for free! During the war in the Gulf, there was a spate of $99 round-trip fares to just about every European destination. However, I have noticed lately that discounts on their "last-minute specials" tend to be far less generous than they once were, especially during the summer.

Once you have flown with Now Voyager a few times, you can ask them to put you on a list for last-minute flights, when you're available to travel on short notice. "We get calls like that all the time," says Ms. Weinberg, and they pay attention, too. "Especially when we get to know them and they become reliable to us — in other words when we know they're really going to follow through and take a flight. We bandy names around the office all the time."

The best way to book or pay for a flight is to go directly to Now Voyager's office. This is especially true if you want to jump on one of their last-minute specials. Take the A, C, E, 1, or 9 subway to Canal Street. Whenever you visit, make sure you bring your passport (and any other travel documents, such as a green card).

Be aware that no New York booking agency's listings precisely match those of the others. To get the fullest selection, you will have to check with all of them.

VEX Wholesale Express (see Air Cargo Partners, above)

World Courier, Inc.
1313 4th Avenue
New Hyde Park, NY 11040
(516) 354-2600

World Courier is an air courier retailer. That means they offer expedited cargo services exclusively to their own roster of business clients.

No longer offering runs to Brussels or Milan, World Courier is now using freelancers to Frankfurt and Mexico City, as follows:

Destination	Departure Days	Length of Stay	Fare Range
Frankfurt	Monday – Thursday	7 - 60 days	$150-$300
Mexico City	Sunday – Thursday	7 days	$100-$200

World Courier's Frankfurt fares are consistently among the best bargains to be found in the air courier business. In addition, World allows couriers to check one bag of up to 40 pounds. Payment must be by cash, certified check, or money order; no credit cards are accepted.

World requires that you have an American or EEC (Common Market) country passport, with a valid "green card" (Permanent Resident Card) in the latter case. Calls for information are accepted Monday through Friday between 9:00 a.m. and 12:00 noon, EST. The courier contact is Barbara Whitting.

You must show up at World's offices (as opposed to the airport) on the day of the flight; you **cannot** leave your car in their lot. They will provide you with information on how to get there through public transportation.

The latest word is that World no longer offers last-minute specials, preferring to use its own staff in emergencies. But World's low, low regular prices are already as good as the last-minute deals offered by other courier companies.

WASHINGTON, DC

The nation's capitol would seem like a natural jumping off point for couriers, and no doubt the diplomatic kind fly off in all directions on a regular basis. Freelance, on-board couriers like you and me, however, are limited to just a few choices.

Air Cargo Partners (ACP)
(a.k.a. VEX Wholesale Express)
Virgin Atlantic Airlines
149-32 132nd Street
JFK International Airport
Jamaica, NY 11430
(888) VEX-MOVE (839-6683)
(718) 529-6814, ext. 4
(718) 529-6817 (Fax)

Air Cargo Partners (ACP) is the in-house courier service for Virgin Atlantic. In addition to their flights from New York to London's Heathrow airport, they also offer the following flight from Washington's Dulles airport.

Destination	Departure Days	Length of Stay	Fare Range
London	Daily	Up to 6 weeks	$430-$510

Consolidator fares can often meet or beat what ACP charges for this run, so shop around. This flight must be booked and paid for through the New York office. On the day of the flight, the courier picks up his or her ticket at the Virgin counter at Dulles. See the New York listing for important information about ACP'S policies and procedures.

Halbart Express
113 Executive Drive
Suite 119

Sterling, VA 20166
(703) 318-6520
(718) 244-7240 (Fax)

Halbart is a New York City-based wholesaler and a major player in the air courier business (see the New York listings for more information about their policies and procedures.)

They maintain an office in northern Virginia, near Washington's Dulles Airport, from which they offer occasional courier flights to London. When available, these flights cost slightly more than the then-prevailing fares on the New York-London run, and involve the same luggage and length-of-stay restrictions.

Despite the Washington, DC departure, all bookings must be made through the New York office.

✈ ✈ ✈ ✈

MIAMI

Miami is a major courier hub to South and Central America. The selection of available destinations changes frequently; at one time or another, every major city in Latin America has been reachable from Miami, along with European destinations like London and Madrid. Unfortunately, one of the larger courier companies, Line Haul, ceased operations recently with the result that far fewer destinations are available than was once the case. It is unclear to what extent, if any, the remaining companies will begin serving Line Haul's old routes. It's not a bad idea to check in regularly with the companies listed below to see what's currently available.

Two local, full-service travel agencies, Martillo Express and Travel, (305) 822-0880, and Time To Go, (305) 885-8505, have booked courier flights in the past, but are no longer doing so.

135

Air Facility
2460 NW 66th Avenue
Building 701, Suite A-270
Miami, FL 33122
Mailing address:
P.O. Box 526426
Miami, FL 33152
(305) 871-4990
(305) 871-7898 (Fax)
email: airfacility@earthlink.net

Air Facility's Miami office (see their New York listing above) is currently offering service to Buenos Aires and Rio. In the past, there was some speculation that they would offer courier flights to Caracas, Lima, and Sao Paulo at a future date. At press time, no decision had been made on whether or not to pick up any of Line Haul's routes.

At press time, Air Facility was offering the following destinations from Miami:

Destination (Airline)	Departure Days	Length of Stay	Fare Range
Buenos Aires (Aero. Arg.)	Mon -Thurs, Saturday	7 - 30 days	$425-$525
Rio de Janeiro (Varig)	Mon - Thurs, Sunday	7 - 30 days	$350

The flight to Rio requires U.S. citizens to travel with a business visa. Air Facility will provide the courier with a letter, which must then be presented to a Brazilian consulate in order to obtain a visa. The consulate in Miami has been charging about $100 for such a visa.

One-way trips are available to Buenos Aires for $400; to Rio the one-way fare is the same as for a round trip. Otherwise, couriers have duties in both directions and are limited to two carry-on bags when flying to Rio. On the Buenos Aires run, courier can take just one carry-on bag on the way down, but can bring two back with them. Flights can be booked up to two months in advance and frequent flyer miles are awarded for both runs. Payment is by money order or cashiers check only. Ingrid Heider handles all courier bookings.

Halbart Express
7331 NW 35th Street
Miami, FL 33122
(305) 593-0260
(305) 593-0158 (Fax)

In the past, Halbart's Miami operation (see their New York listing above) has offered courier service to Buenos Aires, Lima, Madrid, Santiago, Sao Paulo, and Tegucigalpa. Then the list of available destinations dwindled to the following runs:

Destination (Airline)	Departure Days	Length of Stay	Fare Range
London (AA)	Thursday, Friday	7 days	$300-$400
Rio de Janeiro (AA)	Tuesday, Thursday, Friday	Open	$350-$450

Then, Halbart suspended even those flights. At press time, no decision had been made as to whether or not to resume courier service on these runs.

The Miami office had been handling its own bookings, which means they will probably continue to do so if service resumes. Otherwise, check in with the New York office. Policies and procedures at the Miami office were identical to those in New York.

International Bonded Couriers, Inc.
8401 NW 17th Street
Miami, FL 33126-1009
(305) 591-8080

(305) 591-2056 (Fax)
email: ccelis@ibcinc.com
web site: http://www.ibcinc.com

IBC's Miami office uses on-board freelance couriers from time to time. At press time, the following destinations were available to on-board couriers:

Destination (Airline)	Departure Days	Length of Stay	Fare Range
Buenos Aires (Aero. Arg.)	Mon –Thurs, Saturday	7 days	$450
Santiago (LanChile)	Thursday, Saturday	7 days	$450

Service to Caracas, Guatemala, and Kingston (Jamaica) has been discontinued with little chance of resumption, according to information available at press time.

Couriers have duties in both directions and so are restricted to carry-on luggage only in both directions. Bags can be checked for $70 per bag. No frequent flyer miles are awarded on these runs. No return guarantee deposit is required. There are also no last-minute fare reductions, but IBC's year-round $450 fare is extremely reasonable for these destinations to begin with.

Flights can be booked only two or three weeks in advance. Payment is by cash or money order, no checks or credit cards. The courier coordinator is Carolina Celis, who accepts calls between 8:00 a.m. and 3:00 p.m. EST, Monday through Friday.

IBC has offices in Buenos Aires and Santiago that arrange courier flights to Miami (see the Latin America listings). If a courier from one of those cities is returning on a given day, then there is no slot for a Miami courier departing on that date.

At press time, the web site for IBC's Miami office was dedicated solely to letting IBC's customers track their shipments or contact customer service; no courier information was posted.

Lima Services
6115 Johnson Street
Hollywood, FL 33024
(954) 964-8400
(954) 644-1148
(954) 964-0700 (Fax)

Lima Services offers courier service to Lima, Peru on the following schedule:

Destination (Airline)	Departure Days	Length of Stay	Fare Range
Lima (AeroPeru)	Daily	Up to 30 days	$300–$430

Flights leave at 5:30 p.m. The first step to take with Lima Services is to call and ask to be placed on their list. When a flight becomes available, they will call you and begin the booking process. Unfortunately, bookings cannot be made over the phone. You will have to go to their office to firm everything up. Credit cards (Visa) are accepted for payment as well as cash and money orders.

Last-minute openings seem to be available here on a regular basis, with fares dropping to $250 or so. It also may be possible to arrange a flight that originates in Lima.

Contact Gladys for more information, and be prepared to speak Spanish. Some members of the staff speak English, but it will be difficult to make yourself understood.

Trans-Air Systems, Inc.
7264 NW 25th Street
Miami, FL 33122
(305) 592-1771
(305) 592-2927 (Fax)
email: tas@elink.net

Trans-Air is now serving two Latin American destinations, as follows:

139

Destination (Airline)	Departure Days	Length of Stay	Fare Range
Guatemala (AA)	Sunday – Friday	4–30 days	$280-$300
Guayaquil (AA)	Sunday, Tuesday, Wednesday	4–30 days	$220-$260
Quito (AA)	Sunday – Thursday	4–30 days	$250-$300

Flights to Costa Rica, Buenos Aires, Mendoza, Argentina, and Santiago have been discontinued. The higher fares quoted (both above and below) are for the "high" seasons. For Guatemala the high seasons are July and December; for Quito the high seasons are from June 20 through August 15 and from November 22 through January 10.

On the Quito and Guatemala runs, stays of up to a year, can be obtained for a higher fare. The fare for a 60-day stay in Quito is $320-$380, 90 days $480-$495, and one year $675-$725. One-way trips are available for $250-$300. The same fares for Guatemala are $320-$365, $465-$485, and $525-$595. One way fares to Guatemala are $250-$280. Frequent flyer miles can be collected on these flights.

You can also book flights to Miami that originate in Guatemala and Quito (but not Guayaquil). Once again, the length of stay determines the fare, with stays of up to 90 days available. Residents of the United States only can get one-way flights from Guatemala for $260 and from Quito for $320. Bookings and payments for these flights must be made through the Miami office. For more information, see the Latin America section.

While you can pick your own date of return, be aware that you will be limited somewhat because there aren't return flights on every day of the week. Of course, prior bookings can also affect availability. Couriers are restricted to one carry-on bag to

Guatemala and two carry-on bags to Guayaquil and Quito. It is possible to check bags if you are willing to pay the excess baggage fee, which is $45 to Guatemala and $62 to Quito.

Deposits for flights ($50) must be made within five days after making the reservation. Payment in full must be received three weeks before the flight date. They accept cash, certified checks, or money orders. Credit cards are only accepted if it is a last-minute booking.

Bookings can be made up to two months in advance, three months in advance for December. Last-minute fares to Guatemala drop to between $200 and $230. Last-minute openings to Quito are an even better bargain, with fares in the $180 to $200 range. Call Gloria Arauz to book a flight.

✈ ✈ ✈ ✈

DETROIT

Now Voyager
74 Varick Street, Suite 307
New York, NY 10013
(212) 431-1616
(212) 334-5243 (Fax)

Of the booking agencies, Now Voyager seems to have done the best job of keeping on top of courier flights from the minor gateway cities. In the not too distant past, Now Voyager was booking flights from Detroit to Asia. Bangkok, Hong Kong, Singapore, and Tokyo were all available via Northwest at fares that ranged from $586 to $699. On these runs, the courier had the option of returning to JFK in New York as well as to Detroit.

Unfortunately, at press time, these flights were no longer on the menu. However, they are still referred to on Now Voyager's

141

automated attendant at the number above, so these flights may reappear at some point in the future.

When and if they are available, all bookings and payments will be handled through the New York office. See the New York listings for more information about Now Voyager's policies and procedures.

✈ ✈ ✈ ✈

CHICAGO

The mix of courier possibilities out of Chicago has changed once again. Some courier operations have cut back the use of on-board couriers. Travel Headquarters makes it easy for would-be Chicago couriers to reach New York and Miami to take advantage of courier opportunities in those gateways.

Halbart Express
1475 Elmhurst
Grove Village, IL 60018
(847) 806-1250
This is Halbart's Chicago operation. It is now set up to handle bookings, but its only offering at press time was as follows:

Destination (Airline)	Departure Days	Length of Stay	Fare Range
Brussels (AA)	Call	Call	Call

Destination (Airline)	Departure Days	Length of Stay	Fare Range
London (AA)	Monday–Thursday, Saturday	7 or 8 days	$350–$525

The Brussels run was new at press time and details had not been ironed out. On the London run, the Thursday flight requires a stay of eight days. On all other departure days the stay is seven days, except that on the Tuesday and Wednesday flights, the courier has the option to choose a variable stay of from one to 30 days for an extra fee of $75. Couriers are allowed two pieces of carry-on luggage on these runs.

Halbart also has plans to add runs to Frankfurt, Madrid, Paris, and Hong Kong in early 1999. Call for details.

The Chicago office is now handling its own booking arrangements. Call between 9:00 a.m. and 5:00 p.m., Monday through Friday, and ask to speak with booking agents Shereka Williams or Rafael Hernandez. Payment is by certified check or money order only.

See the New York, Miami, and Los Angeles listings for more information on Halbart's courier runs as well as courier policies and procedures.

International Bonded Couriers (IBC)
114 Touhy Court
Des Plaines, IL 60018
(847) 699-3324

IBC has discontinued its flights from the Windy City to Tokyo, Singapore, and Bangkok. When and if they resume, reservations and payments will be handled through their Los Angeles office.

Check the Los Angeles listings for more information on IBC's routes, policies, and procedures.

Jupiter Air, Ltd.
(MICOM America, Inc.)
220 Howard Avenue
Des Plaines, IL 60018
(847) 298-3850
(847) 298-3854 (Fax)
web site: http://www.jupiterair.com

Jupiter's Chicago operation has discontinued its service to London and now offers courier trips to Hong Kong only according to the following schedule:

Destination (Airline)	Departure Days	Length of Stay	Fare Range
Bangkok (JAL)	Sunday – Friday	7 to 30 days	$250-$550
Hong Kong (JAL)	Saturday	10 to 30 days	$250-$550

On the Hong Kong run, couriers must return on a Wednesday. On the Bangkok run, there are no return flights on Saturday or Sunday. Couriers are allotted one checked and one carry-on bag and must post a $100 return-guarantee deposit, which will be returned 14 days after their return. Airport taxes at $40 to Bangkok and $47 to Hong Kong.

There is also an "application fee" levied on first-time Jupiter couriers — $35 to Bangkok and $42 to Hong Kong. Once paid, you can fly from any Jupiter location in the United States for a period of five years without incurring an additional fee. See the Jupiter listings in New York and San Francisco for more information on Jupiter's policies and procedures.

When you are ready to book, you can make your reservation with Elba Mestre. She will send you an application to complete and return with your payment. Elba also maintains a list of emergency couriers for use in the case of last-minute (i.e. two days prior to flight time) availabilities.

144

Travel Headquarters
59 Eisenhower Lane
Lombard, IL 60148
(630) 620-8080
(630) 620-8180 (Fax)

Travel Headquarters is a full-service travel agency that, over the years, has served as a booking agent for a number of courier companies with flights out of Chicago. Recently, they were offering the following destinations:

Destination (Airline)	Departure Days	Length of Stay	Fare Range
Hong Kong (AA, JAL)	Tuesday–Saturday	7 to 30 days	$450–$600
London (AA)	Monday–Thursday,	Up to 30 days	$399–$599

Runs to Brussels, Frankfurt, and Mexico City are no longer available. The trip to Hong Kong requires a refundable $100 deposit; the London trip does not. The London run requires a Saturday night stayover. All flights are restricted to carry-on luggage only.

Call Norm Atkins with the dates you want to travel. Once you have arranged a date, you will receive an application which you must return with your payment. You can book "up to three or four months" in advance. If your flight is more than three weeks away, you can pay by personal check. Otherwise, it's cashier's check or money order. Travel Headquarters does not take credit cards.

In addition to handling these Chicago courier trips, Travel Headquarters can book you on any Halbart courier flight out of New York or Miami and arrange for your connecting flight from Chicago. The add-on fares range from $100 to $175 depending on the destination. Call Norm for a quote. See the New York and Miami listings for more information on Halbart's destinations, policies, and procedures.

UTL Travel
320 Corey Way
South San Francisco, CA 94080
(415) 583-5074
(415) 583-9420 (Fax)

San-Francisco-based travel agency UTL also books courier flights from Chicago to Bangkok and Hong Kong as follows:

Destination (Airline)	Departure Days	Length of Stay	Fare Range
Bangkok (JAL)	Call	Up to 30 days	$535-$565
Hong Kong (JAL)	Call	Up to 30 days	$535-$565

These would appear to be the Jupiter flights listed above. See the San Francisco listings that follow for more information on UTL's policies and procedures.

✈ ✈ ✈ ✈

SAN FRANCISCO

Air Cargo Partners (ACP)
(a.k.a. VEX Wholesale Express)
Virgin Atlantic Airlines
149-32 132nd Street
JFK International Airport
Jamaica, NY 11430
(888) VEX-MOVE (839-6683)
(718) 529-6814, ext. 4
(718) 529-6817 (Fax)

Air Cargo Partners (ACP) is the in-house courier service for Virgin Atlantic. In addition to their flights from New York to London's Heathrow airport, they also offer the following flight from San Francisco.

Destination	Departure Days	Length of Stay	Fare Range
London	Daily	Up to 6 weeks	$540-$660

Consolidator fares can often meet or beat what ACP charges for this run, so shop around. This flight must be booked and paid for through the New York office. On the day of the flight, the courier picks up his or her ticket at the Virgin counter at the San Francisco International airport. See the New York listing for information about ACP'S policies and procedures.

Airhitch
870 Market Street, #1056
San Francisco, CA 94109
(800) 834-9192
(415) 834-9192

This is the San Francisco office of a student-run operation specializing in ultra-low-cost flights to Europe. See Airhitch's New York listing for information about policies and procedures. Airhitch flights from cities on the west coast to Europe average $239 each way. They also sometimes offer flights from other cities, such as Chicago, Miami, and Tampa, for $229 each way.

Another program, "Domestic Airhitch," offers low-cost last-minute fares from Los Angeles to New York and from Oakland to Chicago and New York. Fares from Oakland to New York were recently quoted at $119 one-way. Flights from the west coast to Hawaii are also available at the same price. Flights are only available three to five days in advance.

Call the San Francisco office between 10:00 a.m and 5:00 p.m. PST Monday to Friday, or 10:00 a.m. and 2:00 p.m. Saturday for more information.

IBC–Pacific, Inc.
5793 West Imperial Highway
Los Angeles, CA 90045
(310) 665-1760
(310) 665-0247 (Fax)
web site: http://www.ibcpac.com

At the moment, IBC-Pacific offers the following runs from San Francisco:

Destination (Airline)	Departure Days	Length of Stay	Typical Fare
Bangkok (NW)	Tuesday	11 days	$400
	Wednesday	14 days	
	Thursday	14 days	
	Friday	14 days	
	Saturday	10 days	
Manila	Tuesday–Saturday	14 days	$400

These flights must be booked through IBC's Los Angeles office. See the Los Angeles listing for more information on IBC's policies and procedures.

Johnny Air Cargo
37 Saint Francis Square
Daly City CA 94015
(650) 991-7080
(650) 991-7085 (Fax)

This small operation offers flights to Manila from San Francisco International Airport.

Destination (Airline)	Departure Days	Length of Stay	Fare Range
Manila (China, Asiana)	Daily	Up to 6 months	$350–$700

Flights, which depart in the late evening, are on a variety of airlines. China Airlines and Asiana were the airlines of choice at press time, but Johnny has used Philippine Airlines, United, and Northwest in the past. Couriers can book up to two months in advance and pay with cash, check, or credit cards (except Discover). Couriers are restricted to carry-on baggage only in both directions, since they have courier duties on both legs.

The highest fares are for holiday periods such as Christmas. See the New York and Los Angeles listings for information on Johnny's service to Manila from those cities.

Jupiter Air, Ltd.
(MICOM America, Inc.)
839 Hinckley Road, Suite A
Burlingame, CA 94010
(650) 697-1773
(650) 697-7892 (Fax)
email: juasfo@cris.com
San Francisco is Jupiter's main U.S. location; they also have offices in New York, Chicago, and Los Angeles. Out of San Francisco, they currently offer the following flights:

Destination (Airline)	Departure Days	Length of Stay	Fare Range
Bangkok (UA/JAL)	Daily	7-21 days	$420
Manila (JAL)	Daily	7-30 days	$405-$455
Singapore (JAL)	Monday-Saturday	7-30 days	$350-$500

Beijing, London and Singapore are no longer available, with no word on whether they will be resumed any time soon.

The run to Manila features an overnight stop in Tokyo on

the way out and on the way back. Jupiter puts its couriers up in the posh Nikko Narita hotel near the airport and pays for meals. Bangkok couriers are in Tokyo only for about three hours on the outbound leg, but get a room at the Nikko during the twelve hour layover on the way back. Couriers are allowed one checked bag on the Singapore run and two on all the others.

Flights can be booked two months in advance and usually are. If you're interested in Bangkok or Singapore, ask to speak with Sherill Macapagal at extension 216. If you're headed to Manila, ask for Hayley Liu at extension 213. Once you book a flight, they will send you an application, which you must return with the full fare. Personal checks will be accepted if there is time before the flight for the check to clear. Otherwise, they accept cashier's checks or money orders, no credit cards.

All couriers must provide a $250 return-guarantee deposit on the Bangkok and Manila runs, $100 for Singapore. The deposit will be refunded by mail shortly after you return; there is no need to ask for it. First-time couriers must pay a $35 "initiation fee," good for five years, which is valid for travel from any of Jupiter's U.S. locations.

Jupiter has great last-minute specials. The "fare" can be as low as the $20 departure tax. On one visit to the Bay area, I was offered one of these "free" flights to Singapore, which I couldn't take. But I was available to take a flight a few days later to Bangkok for $148 round-trip. They maintain a list of last-minute couriers, but it's always wise to call in.

UTL Travel

320 Corey Way
South San Francisco, CA 94080
(415) 583-5074
(415) 583-9420 (Fax)

UTL is a full-service travel agency and a courier booking agent. One of the runs they offer is operated by their parent company, U-Freight. The others appear to be Jupiter routes. Recently they were offering the following courier destinations in the Far East:

Destination (Airline)	Departure Days	Length of Stay	Fare Range
Bangkok (UA)	Daily	Up to 30 days	$435-$535
Manila (JAL)	Daily	Up to 30 days	$455-$535
Manila (PAL)	Monday– Friday	Up to 30 days	$475-$535

Runs to Beijing, London, and Singapore were not available at press time. There is a one-week minimum stay to all destinations. Couriers are allowed one piece of checked luggage on JAL flights to Singapore and on Philippines Airlines flights to Manila; all other flights allow only one carry-on piece not to exceed 45 inches in any dimension.

All fares will be higher during the summer and at Christmas time. You can book on the phone but your flight will only be secured when payment is received. Payment must be by money order only. UTL accepts bookings up to three months in advance. All runs require a $100 return-guarantee deposit, which is returned to you automatically by mail on your return. When you are ready to book, call Grace Tang at extension 350 or Rosella Thieu at extension 351. They prefer it if you call with definite dates and destinations in mind.

UTL will offer reduced fares if there is a last-minute need for couriers. The fare varies, but it is usually in the $250 range. UTL urges would-be last-minute couriers to provide UTL with their daytime phone numbers. "If we call and get a machine, we erase them from the list because we know we won't hear from them until the next day, and that's to late."

UTL offers discount consolidator fares to Asian destinations. Recently, Hong Kong was available for $595 round-trip. UTL also books flights from Chicago to Bangkok and Hong Kong on JAL. See the Chicago listings for more information.

LOS ANGELES

Air Cargo Partners (ACP)
(a.k.a. VEX Wholesale Express)
Virgin Atlantic Airlines
149-32 132nd Street
JFK International Airport
Jamaica, NY 11430
(888) VEX-MOVE (839-6683)
(718) 529-6814, ext. 4
(718) 529-6817 (Fax)

Air Cargo Partners (ACP) is the in-house courier service for Virgin Atlantic. In addition to their flights from New York to London's Heathrow airport, they also offer the following flight from Los Angeles — on Virgin Atlantic, of course.

Destination	Departure Days	Length of Stay	Fare Range
London	Daily	Up to 6 weeks	$540-$660

Consolidator fares can often meet or beat what ACP charges for this run, so shop around. This flight must be booked and paid for through the New York office. On the day of the flight, the courier picks up his or her ticket at the Virgin counter at the Los Angeles International airport. See the New York listing for important information about ACP's policies and procedures.

Airhitch
100 North Sepulveda Boulevard
El Segundo, CA 90245
(888) 247-4482
(310) 726-5000

This is the Los Angeles office of a student-run operation specializing in ultra-low-cost flights to Europe. See Airhitch's

New York listing for information about policies and procedures. Airhitch flights from cities on the west coast to Europe average $239 each way.

Another program, "Domestic Airhitch," offers low-cost last-minute fares from Los Angeles to New York and from Oakland to Chicago and New York. Fares from LA to New York were recently quoted at $119 one-way. Flights from the west coast to Hawaii are also available at the same price. Flights are only available three to five days in advance.

Call the Los Angeles office between 10:00 a.m and 5:00 p.m. PST Monday to Friday or 10:00 a.m. and 2:00 p.m. Saturday for more information. Also, see the New York listings for more information about Airhitch and its operations.

Air-Tech Ltd.
588 Broadway
Suite 204
New York, NY 10012
(212) 219-7000
(212) 219-0066 (Fax)
email: fly@airtech.com
web site: http://www.airtech.com

This New York courier booking agency also handles a few runs departing from Los Angeles. However, all bookings must be made and paid for through the New York office. See the New York section (above) for important information about Air Tech's policies and procedures.

At press time, Air Tech was offering the following courier destinations from Los Angeles:

Destination (Airline)	Departure Days	Length of Stay	Fare Range
London (AA)	Call	1 to 2 weeks	$500–$700
Manila (UA)	Call	1 to 2 weeks	$600–800

Destination (Airline)	Departure Days	Length of Stay	Fare Range
Sydney (Qantas)	Call	1 to 2 weeks	$700-$900

East-West Express
149-35 177th Street
Jamaica, NY 11434
(718) 656-6246
(718) 656-6247 (Fax)

East-West Express, New York, offers courier runs from LAX to Australia and New Zealand. The run to Australia offers the courier a choice of four final destinations, as shown in the following chart:

Destination (Airline)	Departure Days	Length of Stay	Fare Range
Auckland (Qantas)	Saturday	Up to 30 days	$750-$1000
Brisbane (Qantas)	Tuesday- Saturday	Up to 90 days	$750-$1200
Cairns (Qantas)	Tuesday- Saturday	Up to 90 days	$750-$1200
Melbourne (Qantas)	Tuesday- Saturday	Up to 90 days	$750-$1200
Sydney (Qantas)	Tuesday- Saturday	Up to 90 days	$750-$1200

Couriers from Los Angeles cannot check any bags on the outbound flight. They may check up to two on the return. Although a return date is required on all bookings, the courier may change this date without penalty. All flights must be booked and paid for through the New York office. On the day of departure, the courier picks up his or her ticket at the Qantas check-in counter at LA International Airport.

Couriers to Australia must choose their final destination from among the four cities listed and must return from that city. An Australian visa is required.

The flights to both New Zealand and Australia originate in New York and stop in LA, so the courier can board in either city. It's booked on a first-come, first-served basis, so if a New York courier books a flight on a given day, that day's run is not available to a courier in Los Angeles and vice versa.

Check East-West in the New York listings for more on destinations and fares from New York and their policies and procedures.

Halbart Express
1000 West Hillcrest Boulevard
Inglewood, CA 90301
(310) 417-3048
(310) 417-9792 (Fax)

Halbart's Los Angeles operation has been expanding in some very attractive directions. At the moment they offer the following routes:

Destination (Airline)	Departure Days	Length of Stay	Typical Fare
London (AA, UA)	Tues – Thurs, Saturday	7 or 14 days	$400-$450
Manila (NW)	Tues – Thurs, Saturday	14 days	$450
Sydney (Air New Zealand)	Tuesday, Wednesday, Saturday	14 days	$550-$850

155

The fare to London varies with the length of stay; it's $400 for a seven day and $450 for a 14 day stay. The fares to London remain fairly constant at about these levels throughout the year as do fares to Manila. The length of stay, either seven or 14 days, is carved in stone on these flights, although I am told that Halbart can sometimes be flexible on trips to Manila.

Couriers to London and Sydney are restricted to two carry-on pieces of luggage only; Manila couriers only get one. Payment is by cash, check, or money order. No credit cards or personal checks are accepted. There is no sign-up fee or return guarantee deposit required.

Bookings should be made only through the LA office, which handles no bookings for any other Halbart offices.

IBC-Pacific, Inc.

5793 West Imperial Highway
Los Angeles International Airport
Los Angeles, CA 90045
(310) 665-1760
(310) 665-0247 (Fax)
web site: http://www.ibcpac.com

IBC uses freelance, on-board couriers to several cities in the Orient. Recently, they were offering service to the following destinations:

Destination (Airline)	Departure Days	Length of Stay	Typical Fare
Bangkok (NW)	Monday	7 or 14 days	$400
	Sunday	14 days	
Hong Kong (NW)	Tuesday	13 days	$400
	Wednesday	13 days	
	Thursday	13 days	
	Friday	8 days	
	Saturday	12 days	
	Sunday	14 days	

Destination (Airline)	Departure Days	Length of Stay	Typical Fare
Manila (NW)	Tuesday- Saturday	14 days	$400
Seoul (NW)	Saturday Saturday	14 days 7-28 days	$400

Notes: The day you depart determines your length of stay, except to Manila where the stay is a fixed 14 days.

Singapore, Taipei, and Tokyo have dropped off IBC's list of destinations, with no word on when, or if, they will return. There are also flights to Bangkok and Manila leaving from San Francisco. See the San Francisco listings for the schedule.

Fares don't vary with the season. The current low fares (down 20% since the last edition of this book) reflect the economic downturn in Asia. The schedule of flights (not to mention the fares) given above may change. Check the precise schedule when you call to book.

Couriers are limited to carry-on luggage only, although you may check a bag by paying the airline's excess baggage fee. IBC also requires a stiff $500 "security deposit" by money order, cashier's check or Visa, MasterCard or American Express credit card. You forfeit the fee for any non-performance of your duties under the courier contract; otherwise, the deposit is returned after the trip has been completed.

From time to time, IBC offers last-minute specials — usually due to a cancellation. They tell me these specials are rare during the summer and unheard of at Christmas time.

Your best bet is slower travel months like February or October. Fares may be reduced to half-price or $100. I know of some couriers who report flying free with IBC during the off-season. Upgrades to Business or First Class are not allowed.

Call between the hours of 9:00 a.m. and 4:00 p.m. PST, Monday through Friday, to get more information and book a flight. They will send you a complete packet of information about their policies and procedures. During other times, the number carries a recorded message giving current destinations (but no information on fares or flight availability). Their web site, however, has a great deal of information about schedules and fares, as well as policies and procedures.

Couriers have duties in both directions and, once booked, the return date cannot be changed for any reason. Unlike many other courier companies, IBC-Pacific requires that its couriers be at least 21 years of age (not 18). In addition to a valid passport, IBC requires its couriers to have a drivers license ("for ID purposes only"). Couriers are also expected to dress neatly and refrain from drinking alcohol before or during their flights.

Johnny Air Cargo

203 South Vermont Avenue
Los Angeles, CA 90004
(213) 386-7080
(213) 386-7277 (Fax)

This friendly cargo service offers courier runs to Manila "three or four times a week" on Korean Airlines. The round-trip fare was $450 when I inquired but goes to a high of $850 during holiday periods. Usually it is in the $500 range. Stays of two or three months are possible. You serve as a courier in both directions and are restricted to carry-on luggage only. They accept credit cards and require a $250 return security deposit.

Jupiter Air, Ltd.
(MICOM America, Inc.)

460 South Hindry Avenue
Unit D
Inglewood, CA 90301
(310) 670-1197
(310) 670-1198
(310) 649-0621 (Fax)
email: jualax@cris.com

Jupiter's Los Angeles operation currently offers the following destinations:

Destination (Airline)	Departure Days	Length of Stay	Fare Range
Bangkok (JAL)	Daily	7–30 days	$400–$450
Hong Kong (JAL)	Daily	7–30 days	$400–$500
Seoul (Asiana)	Tuesday – Saturday	7–30 days	$350–$400
Singapore (UA)	Daily	7–30 days	$400–$500

The runs to Singapore and Hong Kong require a stopover in Tokyo's Narita airport. On the Singapore run, it's just a change of planes, but on the Hong Kong run you will have to clear customs, since some of the baggage you are accompanying is destined for Japan. Jupiter provides its couriers with very detailed and specific instructions on how to do this; you should have no problems if you have the common sense to follow their instructions to the letter.

Since Singapore is a jumping off place for other Southeast Asian destinations, Jupiter asks its couriers to keep them posted on their travel arrangements if they leave Singapore.

Jupiter tells me that the fare code on the tickets they buy from United does not allow frequent flyer miles. All the tickets I have held while flying as a Jupiter courier are stamped "NO AIRLINES MILEAGE."

All Jupiter flights from LA now allow carry-on luggage only. You must also provide a $200 return-guarantee deposit and pay a $35 "initiation fee," good for five years, which is valid for travel from any of Jupiter's U.S. locations. Payment is by cash, certified check, or money order. No credit cards are accepted.

If you are available to fly at the last minute and they have an opening, they will reduce their fares by 50% or more. On a recent visit to Los Angeles, I was offered a $150 round-trip to Seoul. Ask to speak with Kim or Naomi in the booking department when you're ready to book. Call between 9:00 a.m. and 3:30 p.m. Pacific Standard Time.

Jupiter's office in Hong Kong offers the possibility of reaching other Pacific Rim destinations as a courier out of Los Angeles. However, you will have to make separate arrangements with the Hong Kong office for any continuing flights. Obviously, you will have to arrange to be back in Hong Kong in time to catch your return flight to LA. See the "Pacific Rim" chapter for more information about Jupiter's Hong Kong operation. Also, check the San Francisco listings for information on Jupiter flights originating there.

Now Voyager
74 Varick Street, Suite 307
New York, NY 10013
(212) 431-1616
(212) 334-5243 (Fax)
web site: http://www.nowvoyagertravel.com

Now Voyager, the New York booking agent, also books a number of flights from Los Angeles, all of which must be booked through their New York office:

Destination (Airline)	Departure Days	Length of Stay	Fare Range
Auckland (QA, ANZ)	Call	Up to 3 months	Call
Sydney (QA, ANZ) Zealand)	Tuesday, Call	Up to Up to 3 months	Call

The Sydney run allows the courier to choose Sydney, Melbourne, Brisbane, or Cairns as the final destination. Flights must be booked in New York. If East-West doesn't show a particular date as open, Now Voyager might and vice versa.

160

EUROPE

For the courier, Europe effectively means England, since there are very few courier opportunities outside of London. In this chapter then, I have arranged the listings by city as follows — London and Paris. I then mention the space-available opportunities available from several cities on the continent.

LONDON

After New York, London is probably the main jumping-off point for international courier travel. However, in recent years there has been considerable consolidation and shrinkage in the London courier scene. For one thing, the increasing economic and political integration of Europe has lessened the need for courier service to the continent. For another, the growing boom in the Far East, specifically Hong Kong, coupled with lower costs in that region, means that flights that used to originate in London now originate in Hong Kong.

One of the nicest things about London courier flights is that virtually all flights allow checked luggage (although sometimes at a modest fee). For Americans who have chafed under the restrictions of the "carry-on only" rule, this will come as a pleasant surprise. On the downside, courier fares from London have been creeping upward.

161

Several British couriers have told me that the fares offered by London's courier companies, especially to the United States, are not that much lower than those offered by the "bucket shops" in London and elsewhere in Britain. These are consolidators (see page 55) and charter operators who specialize in discount air fares.

The following list will get you started. These contacts have been culled from advertisements. I have no personal experience of any of these operations and, naturally, cannot vouch for their reliability. Caveat emptor.

Classic Travel	(0171) 499--9953
Condor Travel	(0171) 373-0495
Farnley Travel	(0171) 490-7822
FlightBookers	(0171) 757-2444
Galaxy Travel	(0181) 925-0055
STA Travel	(0171) 361-6161/6262
Trailfinders	(0171) 938-3366
Travel Arcade	(0171) 734-5873
Travel Zone	(0171) 287-8997

If you are beginning your travel from England, you may want to check out these discount fares. If the difference is only a few pounds, they might be worth taking for the added convenience of choosing specific dates of departure and return. On the other hand, if your time is flexible, you may want to wait for the deeper discounts offered on last-minute courier flights.

Dedicated British travelers — and I use the word "traveler" in the sense of one who goes abroad for an extended period of time — may want to consider using bucket shops to get a cheap fare to the U.S. that doesn't restrict you to a two- to six-week stay. Then, you can take advantage of occasional last-minute specials to pop back to the proverbial sceptered isle to visit Mum or re-plenish the exchequer. Also, as you tour the United States, you can take advantage of courier flights from Miami, Los Angeles, or other gateway cities to expand your travel horizons even further.

If you are arriving from America, these bucket shops can be a source of cheap fares to other European destinations. Many of them offer attractive fares and vacation packages to destinations in Spain, Portugal, Cyprus, and elsewhere in the Mediterranean that are popular with British vacationers.

[*Important Note:* To dial direct to London from the United States first dial (011) which tells the phone company you are making an international call. Then dial (44), which is England's "country code." Then dial the listed numbers, but omit the initial zero, which is used only in the UK.]

Note: Fares are quoted in pounds sterling. Recently, the pound was trading at approximately .59 to the US dollar.

Air Cargo Partners
(a.k.a. VEX Wholesale Express)
Unit 8, Radius Park
Faggs Road
Feltham, Middlesex TW14 0NG
(0181) 897-5130
(0181) 897-5133 (Fax)

This is the in-house courier operation of Virgin Atlantic Airlines. Recently, they were offering the following international destinations:

Destination	Departure Days	Length of Stay	Fare Range
Hong Kong	Daily	Up to 3 months	£399-£599
Johannesburg	Daily (ex. Tuesday)	Up to 3 months	£399-£499
Los Angeles	Daily	Up to 6 weeks	£255-£399
Melbourne	Tuesday, Friday	Up to 3 months	£575-£699
Miami	Daily	Up to 6 weeks	£255-£399

Destination	Departure Days	Length of Stay	Fare Range
New York	Twice daily	Up to 6 weeks	£180-£310
Newark	Daily	Up to 6 weeks	£205-£310
San Francisco	Daily	Up to 6 weeks	£255-£399
Sydney	Daily (ex. Tues, Fri)	Up to 3 months	£575-£699
Tokyo	Daily (ex. Wed)	Up to 3 months	£499-£550
Washington	Daily	Up to 6 weeks	£205-£310

All prices include security charges, but not travel insurance. Payment can be by check or credit card. Flights can be booked up to three months in advance. No frequent flyer miles are allowed on these flights ("due to the value of the ticket") and since Virgin runs the operation they mean what they say. Couriers are allowed one checked bag weighing up to 23 kilos on these flights. Couriers only carry documents on the JFK and Tokyo runs; on all other flights, courier travel is just like "regular" travel.

Runs to the United States require a two- or three-day minimum stay, while all other routes require a five-day minimum stay. One-way tickets are available to Sydney and Melbourne (£355 to £399) and to Tokyo (£299 to £325).

ACP will discount tickets somewhat at the last-minute — Tokyo can be as low as £400, for example. October and November offer the best chances for a bargain. The courier contact is Stuart Martin.

ACP is known by many couriers by its old name, VEX Wholesale Express. The UK office, however, has begun referring to itself as ACP, or some variant thereof. One document I received from them referred to the company as ACP Wholesale Express, ACP Worldwide, and ACP Express, all on the same page. Some documents you receive from them may refer to Air Cargo Partners. Checks to pay for your flight will also have to be made payable to ACP.

Bridges Worldwide Wholesale Express
Old Mill House, Mill Road
West Drayton, Middlesex UB7 7EJ
(0189) 546-5065
(0189) 546-5100 (Fax)
email: tickets@bridgesww.com
web site: http://www.bridgesww.com

A former ground handling agent for Virgin Atlantic, Bridges now runs its own network of courier services under the leadership of Keith Madden. Routes are as follows:

Destination (Airline)	Departure Days	Length of Stay	Fare Range
Beijing (Lufthansa)	Tuesday, Wednesday, Thursday, Saturday	7 days– 3 months	£350–£499
Osaka (Swissair, Lufthansa)	Tuesday, Thursday, Saturday	7 days– 3 months	£450–£580
Seoul (Lufthansa)	Tuesday– Saturday	7 days– 3 months	£350–£499
Tokyo (Finnair, Swissair)	Tuesday– Sunday	7 days– 3 months	£450–£580

All runs require a minimum stay of 7 days, with a flexible return of up to 30 days subject to availability. The flights to Tokyo and Osaka involve a stop and change of planes in either Frankfurt or Helsinki, depending on the carrier; no stopovers, however.

All these flights can be booked up to three months in advance. Bridges accepts cash, check, Visa, and MasterCard. They require no return-guarantee deposit, but no frequent flyer miles are given on any of their flights.

The courier has duties only on the outbound leg of all runs and will be carrying paperwork. However, all Bridges flights allow the courier one checked bag weighing up to 23 kilos.

British Airways Travel Shops (BATS)
First Floor, Export Cargo Terminal S126
World Cargo Centre (S126)
Heathrow International Airport
Hounslow, Middlesex TW6 2JS
(0181) 564-7009
(0181) 562-6177 (Fax)

This is the on-board courier booking operation for British Airways' in-house courier service. In the past, they offered some 35 courier destinations, reflecting British Airways' extensive international network of routes. Recent changes in customs regulations at many destinations, however, mean that on-board couriers are no longer required, so the list of destinations has shrunk considerably. At press time, they were serving the following destinations:

Destination	Flights/ Week	Length of Stay	Fare Range
Boston	6	Up to 14 days	£130-£195
Budapest	6	Up to 14 days	£60-£90
Buenos Aires	3	Up to 14 days	£320-£480
Chicago	6	Up to 14 days	£130-£195

Destination	Flights/ Week	Length of Stay	Fare Range
Mauritius	3	Up to 14 days	£375-£510
Mexico City	3	Up to 14 days	£300-£450
Miami	6	Up to 14 days	£150-£225
New York	28	Up to 14 days	£130-£195
Philadelphia	6	Up to 14 days	£100-£150
San Francisco	6	Up to 14 days	£150-£225
Seattle	6	Up to 14 days	£150-£225
Tokyo	6	Up to 14 days	£385-£525
Washington	6	Up to 14 days	£100-£150

All prices include tax and basic travel insurance. Be aware, however, that this insurance does not cover cancellation fees, which can be hefty (see below). The fares cited represent the typical yearly range. Calling the main number gives you access to a recorded message giving the current fares (but not availability) for all destinations, as well as any special offers.

The Buenos Aires and Mauritius flights leave from Gatwick, as do some of the flights to New York and Miami. Make sure to check on the departure airport when you book.

There is no minimum stay on any of these runs and you can pick your own date of return, subject to availability, within the 14 day maximum. Changes in return dates, once chosen, are "not possible under any circumstances." However, if "due to exceptional circumstances you can be rescheduled" more than 30 days prior to the flight, changes will be permitted with an "amendment fee." Better not to ask.

BATS likes to book two to three months in advance, although seats are frequently available on shorter notice. Discounts on last-minute flights are decided on a case by case basis. You can book by phone, in fact that is the preferred method. If you are booking from the United States, you can use the fax number, which is advisable since the waits on hold can be lengthy. Simply send a short fax indicating your preferred destination and dates; they will respond. UK-based couriers, however, should restrict themselves to the phone. Payment can be by credit card, and the reservation is only secured with payment in full. Once you have booked, you will be sent a confirmation document which you must present to the BATS representative when you meet him on the day of the flight. Failure to do so may mean that you will have to purchase a full-fare ticket. Couriers can expect to carry a document pouch on most if not all flights. Couriers are allowed to check one bag weighing up to 23 kilos in addition to one carry-on.

One-way flights are available (you serve as a courier only on the outbound leg) but they cost the same as a round trip. No frequent flyer miles are awarded on these flights and, since it's an in-house operation, there's probably not much point to asking anyway.

BATS is less strict on its courier dress code than it used to be but couriers are still expected to "dress smartly." Jogging shorts and trainers (that's sneakers for you Yanks) are taboo, but they now allow jeans if they are "smart" — that is, neatly pressed and not frayed or torn.

Ms. Maddie Sisodiya is the administrator and travel consultant; the manager is Mrs. Claire Hatchwell. Bookings are accepted Monday through Friday from 9:00 a.m. to 5:00 p.m.

Jupiter Air (UK) Ltd.
Jupiter House
Horton Road, Colnbrook
Slough, Berkshire SL3 0BB
(0175) 368-9989
(0175) 368-1661 (Fax)

Courier service by Jupiter to New York has been thrown into a cocked hat by the Federal Aviation Administration's (FAA) insistence on strict rules regarding the handling of courier cargo shipped on U.S. flag carriers. According to the FAA each piece of a courier shipment must be *individually* x-rayed. While Jupiter routinely x-rays entire pouches of cargo (each one of which may contain up to 50 or 60 individual pieces), they feel that complying with U.S. regulations would be economically impossible. One alternative would be to use a British airline, but Virgin and British Airways have their own in-house operations. And using a European flag carrier is out, too, since none of them have direct flights from England to the United States. So the New York run listed below is on hold indefinitely, although I am told that when and if the FAA problem is ironed out they will resume the run.

Destination (Airline)	Departure Days	Length of Stay	Fare Range
New York (AA)	Monday – Saturday	7 or 28 days	£150-£220
Sydney (JAL)	Daily	Up to 3 months	@£550

Flights to San Francisco and Tokyo have been discontinued. One reason the Tokyo flight is a thing of the past is that the Sydney courier does double duty as the Tokyo courier during a stopover at Tokyo's Narita airport en route to Sydney. One ways to Sydney are sometimes available for about £300.

Couriers are allowed to check one bag of no more than 20 kilos on these flights. Bookings are accepted up to three months in advance. Upon booking, they will send you an application form to be filled out and returned. Payment can be by check, cash, or credit card. As with Jupiter's flights from the United States, no frequent flyer mileage is awarded on these runs. The courier contact is Jonathon Hearne; call between 9:00 a.m. and 2:00 p.m.

Line Haul Express, Ltd.
Building 252, Section D
Ely Road
London Heathrow Airport
Hounslow, Middlesex TW6 2PR
(081) 759-5969
(081) 759-5973 (Fax)

All of Line Haul's flights now originate in Hong Kong. See the Pacific Rim chapter for more details.

Nomad Courier Service
664 Hanworth Road
Hounslow, Middlesex TW4 5NP
(0181) 893-3820
(0181) 898-2117 (Fax)

This operation is affiliated with New York's Halbart Express. Recently they were offering the following destination from London:

Destination (Airline)	Departure Days	Length of Stay	Fare Range
New York (AA)	Monday – Saturday	1-2 weeks	£125-£280

At press time, this run had been suspended due to the same contretemps with the FAA that halted Jupiter's U.S.-bound service (see above). The folks at Nomad tell me they hope to have the problem solved by late 1998 or early 1999. But of course there are no guarantees:

The fare range listed reflects the winter (January, February) low and the summer (July, August) high. During the other months, fares can be £150, £200, or £250. Bookings can be made quite easily over the phone using a major credit card for payment.

While couriers are restricted to carry-on luggage on this run, it is possible to check up to two bags for the modest fee of £10 each. The courier contact is Christopher Alty.

PARIS

There is only one true air courier left in Paris — Halbart, which is listed below. If they can't get you to the States, you might want to try the Paris office of Air-Tech (below) or Airhitch, which is listed under "Other European Contacts" on the following page.

Note: Fares are quoted in French Francs. recently, the franc was trading at approximately 5.8 to the US dollar.

Blue Marble Travel
(Air-Tech)
2, rue Dussoubs
75002 Paris
(33) (1) 42-36-92-76
(33) (1) 42-21-14-77 (Fax)

This is the European contact for Air-Tech's space-available flights to the United States. They operate in much the same fashion as Airhitch. See the New York listings for important information about Air-Tech's policies and procedures.

You can also call or fax Air-Tech's New York office when making arrangements for your return flight from Europe.

Halbart Express
85, avenue Gabriel Peri
92120 Montrouge
Paris
(33) (1) 46-56-32-32
(33) (1) 46-56-57-28 (Fax)

A reader in Switzerland informs me that Halbart is now flying to New York, on American Airlines. The fare is a very reasonable 1,500FF, but with a 3,000FF security deposit.

Flights leave Thursday and Saturday only. A very attractive feature of this run is that it features an open return, which effectively means a stay of up to one year. Ask for Mina.

OTHER EUROPEAN CONTACTS

Airhitch

Airhitch has a number of European offices, which are listed below. Airhitch can provide you with vouchers for space-available travel to the United States. They will try to get you a flight from the city in which the office is located but do not guarantee that they will be able to do so. You may have to travel to another European city to get a flight. You may have to call first to make an appointment to come into the office. Some of the phones listed have an automated attendant offering recorded information. Airhitch is not a courier company. See the New York listings for important information on Airhitch's policies and procedures.

Airhitch has offices in a number of major European cities, as follows:

Amsterdam, Netherlands	(31) (20) 623-2977
Berlin, Germany	(49) (30) 440-8687
Bonn, Germany	(49) (228) 97-35-222
Madrid, Spain	(34) (1) 541-3083
Paris, France	(33) (1) 47-00-16-30
Prague, Czech Republic	(42) (2) 2422-9536
Rome, Italy	(39) (6) 7720-8655

The Paris office is open year-round; the other offices operate seasonally, during the peak summer travel months.

PACIFIC RIM

This chapter covers the burgeoning courier scene in the nations of the Pacific Rim, including Australia and New Zealand.

The level of courier activity is a function of economic vitality, and thanks to the so-called "Asian Miracle," courier travel boomed in the region in recent years, with most of the growth concentrated in the economic powerhouses of Hong Kong and Singapore. While the more recent "Asian Contagion" of economic woes has put bit of a dent in Pacific Rim courier flights, it has also created some real bargains for those carrying strong currencies.

This listing is arranged alphabetically by country, then by company name.

✈ ✈ ✈ ✈

AUSTRALIA

Courier travel from Australia continues to shrink, not because of economic problems but because of operating efficiencies. For example, changes in customs regulations no longer require the use of an on-board when shipping expedited cargo to New Zealand, so TNT Express Worldwide and Jupiter (below) no longer nave a need for casual couriers to Auckland. That means Jupiter, with its London flight, is the only game in town. And word is that even that run may soon be able to operate without an on-board!

Note: All fares are quoted in Australian dollars. Recently, the Australian dollar was trading at approximately 1.7 to the US dollar.

Jupiter Air Oceania, Ltd.
Unit 3, 55 Kent Road
Mascot, New South Wales 2020
Australia
(61) (2) 9317 2230
(61) (2) 9317 2238 (Fax)
Jupiter's courier service from Australia continues to shrink. At present their only run is:

Destination (Airline)	Departure Days	Length of Stay	Fare Range
London (Qantas/JAL)	Monday – Saturday	2 weeks to 2 months	A$1100 – A$1550

This flight goes out on either Qantas or Japan Air Lines and returns on JAL. A two week minimum stay is required. One-way tickets are no longer available. These flights allow 20 kilos of checked luggage.

Jupiter begins taking bookings three months in advance and apparently the slots fill up fast. Courier Coordinator Robert

174

Rogan only uses couriers from the Sydney area on this run, so there's not much point in calling from overseas, or even from elsewhere in Australia. Jupiter cannot and will not answer questions they receive by fax. However, if you're in Australia — and are going to be there long enough to book a flight three months out — call Robert to make arrangements.

✈ ✈ ✈ ✈

HONG KONG

Hong Kong seems to have shaken off whatever nervousness there may have been about the reversion to Chinese sovereignty in July of 1997. Just one sign of the enclave's renewed self-confidence is the fact that the courier business in the former British colony has remained remarkably robust. Hong Kong is still the undisputed number-one courier hub of the Pacific Rim.

Hong Kong courier flights can be booked from abroad, but, unless you have a local bank account, you will typically have to obtain a bank draft payable in Hong Kong dollars to seal the deal. Factor the cost of this, as well as any expedited shipping costs for getting the draft to Hong Kong, when you make your travel plans.

Note: All fares are quoted in Hong Kong dollars. Recently, the Hong Kong dollar was trading at approximately 7.74 to the US dollar.

Aeronet Express Hong Kong
Room 315
Air Courier Terminal Office Building
Hong Kong International Airport
Kowloon, Hong Kong
(852) 2751-6186
(852) 2755-8467 (Fax)

This company offers some South East Asian destinations that are hard to come by from other courier sources. At press time, their roster of flights was as follows:

Destination	Departure Days	Length of Stay	Fare Range
Jakarta	Tuesday – Friday	Up to 3 months	HK$2300– HK$2800
Kuala Lumpur	Tuesday – Friday	Up to 1 month	HK$2300– HK$2750
London	Tuesday – Friday	Up to 1 year	HK$4200– HK$6000
Singapore	Monday	14 days – 1 month	HK$1985– HK$2385

All flights are on Singapore Airlines and you can accumulate frequent flyer miles. You pick up your ticket at the airport an hour before departure and function as a courier only on the outbound leg, but there is no pouch to carry and no one to meet at the destination. Couriers are restricted to carry-on only on the outbound leg but have the full luggage allotment on their return, since they are not functioning as a courier on this leg. You can pay the excess baggage fee to check a bag on the outbound leg, but I am told this is very expensive. Another nice feature is that the courier receives the return ticket on the departure date. The return date on these tickets can be changed with no penalty.

Most flights have morning departures. The Singapore run has both morning and evening departures, with a dual price structure. Morning flights cost HK$2,385 and allow a stay of up to 1 month, while evening flights cost HK$1,985 and allow a stay of up to 14 days. So, if you plan on being in Singapore less than two weeks, be sure to book the cheaper flight.

Flights can be booked two months in advance. A refundable deposit of HK$1,000 is required on all flights. Payment is by cash or Hong Kong dollar check only. All bookings can be handled by phone and there is no need to go to Aeronet's office, unless perhaps to make a payment. If you do go, take the MTR to the Kowloon Bay station and hail a taxi. The staff canteen on the 6th floor serves excellent and very cheap meals. The courier contact is Ernest Y. K. Tse, the Station Manager.

Atlas Express
Room 2302-3 Fook Lee Commercial Centre
33 Lockhart Road
Wanchai, Hong Kong
(852) 2529-9123
(852) 2528-3010 (Fax)
email: buster@hkstar.com

This boutique operation was offering a run to Taipei, daily except Sunday on China Air for a fare of HK$1,300, plus a return-guarantee deposit of HK$2,000. There was a minimum stay of three days and a maximum of 60 days.

Unfortunately, at press time, they had discontinued this service. Too bad. I took this run and it was a great bargain, and the people at Atlas a lot of fun to work with. If they reinstate service, bookings may be handled through Lotus Tours (see separate listing).

If you have reason to contact Atlas directly, you will find the Manager, Robert Wong, to be extremely friendly and helpful. He lived many years in San Francisco and speaks flawless English.

Bridges Worldwide
Room 8, 9th floor
Pacific Trade Center
2 Kai Hing Road
Kowloon Bay, Hong Kong
(852) 2305-1412/3
(852) 2795-8312 (Fax)
email: 101776.556@compuserve.com
web site: http://www.bridgesww.com

The Hong Kong branch of Bridges offers frequent service to Bangkok at attractive fares, along with the only courier runs to

San Francisco and Sydney. Recently, they were offering the following destinations:

Destination (Airline)	Departure Days	Length of Stay	Fare Range
Bangkok (Thai, Canadian Qantas, Airlanka)	Daily	Up to 90 days	HK$1000– HK$1200
San Francisco (Singapore)	Monday – Thursday	Open	HK$3800– HK$5500
Sydney (Qantas)	Tue-Thurs, Saturday	6–60 days	HK$6800– HK$7000

The schedule to Bangkok is rather complicated, with two flights on some days, and changes with the seasons, so call to confirm the schedule when you're ready to travel. Only the flight on Airlanka (Saturday only at press time) allows the courier to stay up to 90 days; flights on the other airlines offer a maximum stay of 21 days. The day of the week on which you can return from Bangkok also varies with the airline flown.

Couriers are allowed to check one 20-kilo bag on all flights, except one-way trips to San Francisco. Couriers on the Sydney run can arrange to return from Sydney, Brisbane, or Melbourne. All couriers are responsible for paying the HK$50 departure tax and U.S.-bound couriers must pay the HK$290 U.S. tax.

Flights may be booked up to three months in advance. For the more expensive flights, they will ask for a deposit of half the fare, with the remainder due a few weeks prior to departure. There is a HK$2,000 return guarantee deposit for the Bangkok flight but none for the others. I am told that, if you will be returning to the United States as a courier (and therefore have to return to Hong Kong to get your ticket), they will waive the deposit for the Bangkok run on the theory that you are a good risk.

Since the courier only functions as such on the outbound leg, Bridges will issue one-way tickets. The prices are HK$700 to

Bangkok, HK$2,000 to HK$2,800 to San Francisco and HK$4,000 to HK$4,200 to Sydney.

The very friendly Craig Wootten, who is General Manager of the branch, tells me that they almost never have problems filling the Sydney run with Aussies returning home. Even if they lose a courier, they can arrange to send their cargo to Sydney without a courier, so there are never any last-minute bargains available on this run. To Bangkok, however, even though there are some regulars who make the run nearly every week, they occasionally need a last-minute courier. The San Francisco run, too, seems to have more than its share of empty slots. Prices go down as flight date approaches and "we give away the odd freebie," says Wootten.

When you're ready to book, the courier contacts are Jeanne Wong and Candy Chung. Bridges' offices are located near the airport cargo area. The best way to get there, should you need to, is to take the MTR to the Kowloon Bay station and hail a taxi.

Dyna-Trans (Hong Kong) Limited

5th Floor, 152 Queens Road
Central, Hong Kong
(852) 2805-1551
(852) 2545-0165 (Fax)
email: courier@dyna-trans.com
web site: http://www.dyna-trans.com

This office is affiliated with Air Cargo Partners (a.k.a. VEX Wholesale Express) and books couriers to London only. Flights operate daily on Virgin Atlantic. All flights are non-stop, with a departure late in the evening. The fare varies from HK$5,000 to HK$6,600, usually toward the higher end of this range. There is a maximum stay of 45 days. The courier has no specific duties on this run other than occupying the seat. You meet the Dyna-Trans rep a few hours prior to flight time to get your ticket; 20 kilos of checked luggage is allowed in both directions.

A "Courier Application Form" is on their web site and can be submitted electronically. The courier coordinator is Gloria Tse. Mr. Harry Ip is the ACP representative.

Jupiter Air, Ltd.

Suite 1701, Tower One
China Hong Kong City
33 Canton Road
Kowloon, Hong Kong
(852) 2735-1946
(852) 2735-1886
(852) 2735-0450 (Fax)
email: eve@ccmgate.juahkg.com
web site: http://www.jupiterair.com

This impressive Kowloon office, with its marble floors and panoramic view of Hong Kong island, is Jupiter Air's world headquarters. Recently, Jupiter was offering the following selection of destinations:

Destination (Airline)	Departure Days	Length of Stay	Typical Fare
Chicago (JAL)	Wednesday	Up to 30 days	HK$5,000
Los Angeles (JAL)	Daily	Up to 30 days	HK$4,000
New York (UA)	Monday – Saturday	Up to 30 days	HK$5,500
Singapore (United)	Daily	Up to 30 days	HK$2,100

The London run had been cancelled at press time, with no indication when, if ever, it will resume. Sydney, Tokyo, and Vancouver had dropped off the list earlier. When flying to New York on Japan Air Lines, the courier must overnight in Tokyo, with Jupiter footing the bill. The courier will be carrying a document pouch on all runs except Singapore.

Jupiter requires a HK$1,000 return-guarantee deposit on all flights. All these runs allow at least one checked bag. Flights on

United allow two bags of up to 30 kilos each.

I am told that when they have a need for a last-minute courier, the price can be cut by 50 percent. If they are especially desperate, the flight will be free. These flights tend to go to local couriers who have flown with Jupiter before and are known to be reliable.

Bookings can be made up to two months in advance. Jupiter accepts only cash and checks for payment. It is possible to change your return date prior to departure, but this incurs a penalty of at least 20 percent of the "administration fee" (the fare); the penalty rises the closer to departure date the change is requested. Once the courier has departed, the return date cannot be changed.

I have flown with Jupiter out of Hong Kong and find them a joy to work with. The written instructions they provide are detailed and crystal clear. Ask to speak with Eve Lai or Jovie Chan when you are ready to book.

Jupiter's corporate web site lists their offices around the world, along with limited information on courier flights from the cities where they are available.

Linehaul Express (HK) Ltd.
A division of Cathay Pacific
Unit 9, 22nd Floor, Tower One
China Hong Kong City
33 Canton Road
Tsimshatsui, Kowloon, Hong Kong
(852) 2735-2012
(852) 2735-1372 (Fax)

"Acting as our courier," says Linehaul, "can save you up to 60% of the normal ticket fare whilst enjoying a confirmed seat booking even in peak season."

All booking for Linehaul is now handled by Lotus Tours, Ltd. (see separate listing below). The address and phone numbers above are provided in case, for some unforeseen reason, Lotus stops booking for Linehaul. All inquiries should be directed to Lotus.

Recently, Linehaul was offering the following destinations from Hong Kong:

Destination	Departure Days	Length of Stay	Typical Fare
Bangkok	Sunday – Friday	4–14 days	HK$1450
Manila	Sunday – Friday	up to 2 weeks	HK$1250
Shanghai	Sunday – Friday	2–30 days	HK$1900
Taipei	Sunday – Friday	4–30 days	HK$1300
Tokyo	Sunday – Friday	4–14 days	HK$2500

Flights to Beijing, Frankfurt, London, Manchester, Osaka, Seoul, and Sydney have been discontinued, perhaps a symptom of the Asia-wide economic downturn of 1998.

All flights are on Cathay Pacific and a return–guarantee deposit (or "performance deposit" as they call it) of HK$2,000 is required on all routes. Couriers are allowed carry-on luggage only.

Couriers carry a pouch only on the Bangkok, Shanghai, Tokyo, and Osaka runs. The Bangkok, Shanghai, and Tokyo runs occasionally have last-minute availabilities, in which case the "arrangement fee" (the fare) will be in the HK$800 to HK$1,000 range. Why only these runs? Apparently on the other routes, if they lose a courier, the shipment can still go through with only minimal hassle. The other three routes require the physical presence of a courier.

See the Lotus Tours listing, which follows, for further information on booking and payment procedures for all Linehaul flights.

Lotus Tours, Ltd.
14th Floor, Kai Seng Commercial Center
4-6 Hankow Road
Tsimshatsui, Kowloon, Hong Kong
(852) 2316-1997
(852) 2311-2639 (Fax)

This travel agency has taken over the booking duties for Linehaul Express (see separate listing). They are located in the heart of Tsimshatsui, just a stone's throw from the misnamed Chungking Mansions, of backpacker fame, and right across the street from the Duty Free Shopping complex. The courier operation is located in a separate office through the main reception area.

They accept bookings over the phone, and payment may be made by cash or check. Major credit cards are also accepted, with addition of three percent to the fare. However, if the flight is only two days away, they will accept cash only. If you are booking from overseas, you will need to obtain a bank draft payable in Hong Kong dollars.

Ms. Rosana Leung is the Courier Rostering Supervisor. You can also speak with Matthew Chan or Wendy To.

✈ ✈ ✈ ✈

JAPAN

Considering Japan's vaunted status as the Asian economic powerhouse, it may seem odd that it has relatively little in the way of courier service. One reason is that Japan's geographic location enables shippers there to make use of couriers who originate in either the United States or Hong Kong and whose planes must stop at Narita en route to their final destinations.

Note: All fares are quoted in Japanese yen. Recently, the yen was trading at approximately 140 to the US dollar.

Assist Air Service
[no address provided]
Chiba
(81) (0476) 33-4000
(81) (0476) 33-0411 (Fax)

This operation doesn't like to divulge its address but, judging from the phone number, it is near Narita Airport like the other courier companies. It offers one courier run at a very attractive price, as follows:

Destination (Airline)	Departure Days	Length of Stay	Typical Fare
Hong Kong (NW)	Monday – Friday	up to 90 days	¥30,000

Reservations can be made up to three months in advance, but they will not accept reservations from anyone not in Japan. Payment must be made by direct deposit to their bank account only. No credit cards or checks are accepted. Assist Air Service does not require a return guarantee deposit. Couriers cannot collect frequent flyer miles or fly one-way; they are also restricted to carry-on only.

Air Assist Service will discount the fare when there is a last-minute availability. However, last-minute flights are offered only to those people on a list they maintain. I suspect that if you are not Japanese your odds of being added to the list are slim. However, resident *gaijin* may be considered.

Fastlink Express Inc.
476, Nanaei
Tomisato-machi, Inba-gun
Chiba
(81) (0476) 91-2895
(81) (0476) 91-0313 (Fax)

Fastlink Express has taken over for TNT Express Worldwide. Recently, the following destinations were being offered:

Destination (Airline)	Departure Days	Length of Stay	Typical Fare
Bangkok (NW)	Tuesday	9 days	¥45,000
Hong Kong (NW)	Monday – Saturday	9 days	¥45,000
Singapore (NW)	Tuesday	9 days	¥45,000

Bookings can be made at any time prior to three days before flight time, although they do not discount fares at the last minute. Payments must be made by direct deposit to their bank account. No credit cards are accepted. No return guarantee deposits are required.

Fastlink requires that all couriers have passports with at least six months of validity. All flights require the courier to meet the Fastlink rep at Narita at 4:00 p.m. In the past, some runs allowed checked baggage; the word now is that all runs restrict the courier to carry-on only. Only the Bangkok run requires the courier to carry a pouch and meet a rep at the airport. This usually takes 15 to 20 minutes. Bangkok couriers should bring along photocopies of the ID page of their passport.

On all flights, on-boards function as couriers on the outbound leg only. The courier contact is Akira Kukinono ("Kucky").

Jupiter Japan Co. Limited
2/F, Marusho Building
779-3 Azuma-Cho, Narita-Shi
Chiba
(81) (476) 24-2157
(81) (476) 24-2458 (Fax)
 Jupiter's Japan office does not originate any courier flights,

using couriers in transit from elsewhere. I have listed their office address and phone numbers here for the benefit of Jupiter couriers who might need to contact them in case of an emergency. Ask to speak with Douglas Desper.

Wholesale Courier Network
2-20-14, Tsurumatsu Building 2F, Hiyoshidai
Tomisato-machi, Inba-gun
Chiba
(81) (0476) 92-0311
(81) (0476) 92-0309 (Fax)
Wholesale serves the same destinations as Fastlink, but has suspended its use of on board couriers.

✈ ✈ ✈ ✈

KOREA

Note: Korea's currency went into a nosedive in 1998, and courier flights are now quoted in U.S. dollars, not Korean won.

Jupiter Express Co., Ltd.
663-12 Kong Hang Dong
Kang Suh-Gu
Seoul
(82) (2) 665-6024/5
(82) (2) 665-1777 (Fax)
Recently, Jupiter was reported to be offering two courier runs, as follows:

Destination (Airline)	Departure Days	Length of Stay	Typical Fare
Los Angeles (Asiana)	Daily	Up to 30 days	US$350

Destination (Airline)	Departure Days	Length of Stay	Typical Fare
New York (Asiana)	Daily	Call	Call

Bookings can be made two or more months in advance. There is also a return-guarantee deposit of US$400. Payment can be made in US dollars, or in Korean won at the then-prevailing rate of exchange.

The Seoul-New York run reportedly uses staff couriers, but the occasional opening might be available for a casual courier. The courier is allowed to check one piece of luggage on these run. The courier contact is Mr. Jung, Tong Hyun.

✈ ✈ ✈ ✈

NEW ZEALAND

Note: All fares are quoted in New Zealand dollars. Recently, the New Zealand dollar was trading at approximately 2.02 to the US dollar.

TNT Express Worldwide
6 Doncaster Street
Mangere, Auckland
or P.O. Box 73122
Auckland International Airport
New Zealand
(64) (9) 255-0534
(64) (9) 255-0504

Service to Sydney has been discontinued and is most likely gone forever, now that Australian customs has simplified its procedures for expedited cargo. However, TNT is still offering the following destinations, all via Air New Zealand:

Destination	Departure Days	Length of Stay	Typical Fare
Frankfurt (ANZ)	Call	Up to 1 year	NZ$2300
London (ANZ)	Call	Up to 1 year	NZ$2300
Los Angeles (ANZ)	Monday – Saturday	Up to 2 months	NZ$1450– NZ$1600

Days of departure to London and Frankfurt vary through the year, as Air New Zealand adjusts its schedules from season to season. TNT also offers some attractive options on these flights. If you choose to be a courier both going to and returning directly from Los Angeles, you will pay the lowest fare (NZ$1,200 at press time). For an additional fare (whatever Air New Zealand is charging at the time) you can continue on to other points in the U.S., returning to Los Angeles to resume your courier duties back to Auckland. Under this arrangement, your maximum stay would be two months. For $NZ1,600 you can extend your stay for up to a year. You can also fly one-way to LA, but the fare is only slightly less than the round-trip.

On flights to London and Frankfurt, you are serving as a courier only on the outbound leg. That means you can elect to stop over in either Los Angeles or Honolulu on the return leg at no additional cost. You can also fly one-way for about NZ$1,000 less than the round-trip fare.

Would-be couriers must fill out an application and return it with a copy of their passport. "You will be contacted with confirmation of your dates to travel within two or three days," TNT promises. "Once these dates are provided to you, we will require a deposit of $300 minimum. Final payment is required six weeks prior to departure." The courier contact is Christine Toopi.

✈ ✈ ✈ ✈

SINGAPORE

The Singapore courier scene has been changing. Bridges Worldwide's routes have been taken over by Jupiter's Singapore agent, Air United. TNT has suspended flights, at least for now.

Perhaps your best bet for a trip out of Singapore is to Bangkok. There are several flights each day offered by several companies. Most other trips are inter-Asia, with a few to the United States. Expedited freight to Europe no longer requires the presence of an on-board courier.

Low-cost consolidator airfares and land/sea excursions to nearby Malaysia and Indonesia are advertised daily in *The Straits Times* (60 cents). Look for the "Tours" section at the back of the Classifieds.

By the way, you should have no difficulty dealing in English with any of the companies listed here.

Note: Fares are quoted in Singapore dollars. Recently, the Singapore dollar was trading at approximately 1.77 to the US dollar.

Air United International Pte. Ltd.

150 Orchard Road
Room 05-52, Orchard Plaza
Singapore 238841
(65) 735-7684
(65) 735-7584 (Fax)

This friendly and helpful operation is conveniently located on the fifth floor of a mall in the upscale Orchard Road shopping district. It is the Singapore ground operator for Jupiter and offers Jupiter flights under the Air United name. Recently, the following destinations were being offered:

Destination (Airline)	Departure Days	Length of Stay	Typical Fare
Bangkok (Thai, Singapore)	Daily	Up to 14 days	S$165
Hong Kong (UA)	Daily	Up to 30 days	S$365
Manila (Singapore)	Tues, Thurs Sunday	4 to 30 days	S$500
San Francisco (JAL)	Daily	Up to 30 days	S$900

Flights to Los Angeles and Tokyo have been discontinued. Flights to San Francisco allow one 30-kilo checked bag. To Bangkok, you are allowed carry-on only. For U.S. flights, couriers must post a S$200 return-guarantee deposit. The LA run involves an 11-hour stop in Tokyo, with Jupiter picking up the bill for a hotel room.

None of these runs requires the courier to carry a pouch, however Bangkok-bound couriers must sign some paperwork for Bangkok customs. Although this is, in effect, a Jupiter operation, there is no "membership fee" for first-time couriers.

Bookings can be made a month or so in advance. However, a week to four days before flight date, the fares drop to "half price." On a recent visit to Air United's office, there was a flight available to San Francisco leaving in about four days for S$600 (about $429 US). Speak with Karen Ho when you're ready to book. Everyone in this office speaks excellent English.

Airpak Express Pte. Ltd.
48 MacTaggart Road
Unit 05-04
Singapore 368088
(65) 383-9200

(65) 282-3119
(65) 282-0091 (Fax)
email: airpak.sin@pacific.net.sg

This company operates a courier run to Manila four times a week, on Tuesdays, Wednesdays, Thursdays, and Sundays. They ask that would-be couriers call them about one week before their preferred departure date to inquire about flight availability.

The fare is S$300 and the flight is on Philippine Airlines (flight number PR502). The run departs at 9:40 a.m. and arrives at 1:15 p.m. They accept payment in cash only. Couriers are allowed carry-on baggage only and you cannot check a bag even if you are willing to pay the excess baggage fee. However, since you function as a courier only on the outbound leg, you have a full luggage allotment on the return trip. Couriers carry no pouch and don't have to meet anyone at the Manila airport. Call Jenny Erh when you are ready to book.

If, for some reason, you already hold a ticket to Manila from Singapore on Philippine Airlines, you can call Jenny and volunteer to be their courier. If they need a courier that day, they will pay you up to S$150. In other words, your cost is always S$300. Remember, your ticket must be on Philippine Airlines.

Airpak also operates courier runs to other major Asian cities on an as-requested basis and on a variety of airlines. Call to see what might be available when you are available to travel.

Airtropolis Express
SATS Express and Courier Centre
Cargo Agent Building D
Unit #04-17
Singapore Changi Airport
Singapore 819827
Mailing address: P.O. Box 0877, Singapore 918113
(65) 543-1377; 545-3686
(65) 542-1117; 545-2055 (Fax)

Airtropolis is currently offering two daily flights to Bangkok. Flights to Kuala Lumpur have been discontinued. One flight leaves at about 8:50 a.m. and the other at 10:50 p.m. Most flights are on Singapore airlines and cost S$200 to S$250. However, there are two flights each week, one on SAS and the other on Alitalia, that cost only S$100 to S$150. The minimum stay is four days and the maximum two weeks. If they need a courier on short notice, they have been known to give the ticket away.

This run allows carry-on baggage only. The courier carries no pouch but must meet a courier representative in Bangkok, since Thai customs requires the courier to sign some paperwork. In my experience, this is a simple and painless process. The courier meeting point at the Bangkok airport is well marked (in fact, the sign says "Courier Meeting Point"). On the return leg, the courier meets the rep in Bangkok for check-in but has no duties on arrival back in Singapore.

Airtropolis's flights are booked by Air United (see separate listing), conveniently located in downtown Singapore. Reaching Airtropolis itself is a bit of an adventure. It involves hiring a taxi and getting a police pass to enter the free trade zone of Changi Airport's Air Freight Centre. Should you need to contact Airtropolis directly, Leslie Lim is the Hub Manager, C.M. Ho is the General Manager.

Circle Concord International

Cargo Agent, Building C
Unit 01-06/08
Airport Cargo Road
Singapore
(65) 542-2894
(65) 542-2649 (Fax)

Formerly called Concord Express, this courier operation has been expanding its list of courier runs and, at press time, was offering the following destinations:

Destination (Airline)	Departure Days	Length of Stay	Typical Fare
Bangkok (Finnair, SAS)	Daily	Up to 2 weeks	S$120

Destination (Airline)	Departure Days	Length of Stay	Typical Fare
Kuala Lumpur (Singapore)	Daily	Up to 2 weeks	S$120
Taipei (Singapore)	Daily	Up to 2 weeks	S$120

Bookings should be made on the phone (they discourage would-be couriers from coming to their offices). You will actually pick up and pay for your ticket at Ericson Travel, 298 Beach Road, The Concourse Shopping Mall. The telephone there is (65) 295-4850. Circle Concord International is affiliated with OBC in Bangkok (see Thailand listings).

✈ ✈ ✈ ✈

TAIWAN (REPUBLIC OF CHINA)

The courier scene in Taiwan has been winding down and will no doubt continue to do so. Jupiter has discontinued operations here and TNT has all but stopped. Nonetheless, there are occasionally courier opportunities here

Note: All fares are quoted in New Taiwanese dollars (NT$). Recently, the New Taiwanese dollar was trading at approximately 34.8 to the US dollar.

Linehaul Express Co.
9 Alley 25 Lane
216 Chungsiao East Road, Sec.
Taipei
(886) (2) 741-2610
(886) (2) 781-8315 (Fax)

Linehaul in Taiwan is the ground agent for the Taipei flights IBC sends out of LA. From time to time, they offer flights out of Taipei. During a recent visit, they told me they had suspended their Hong Kong service but that it might start up again.

When available, Taipei-LA flights are on Cathay Pacific at a fare of NT$ 5,500. There is a minimum stay of two nights and a maximum of 55 days. If you'd like to check out the possibilities, contact Ms. Irene Lee.

TNT Skypak International
B.V. Taiwan Branch
3rd floor
207 Tun Hua North Road
Taipei
(886) (2) 713-2345, ext. 262
(886) (2) 712-2234 (Fax)

TNT reportedly has a very occasional need for an on-board courier to Tokyo. Flights are rare but, if you want to try, the courier contact is David Shu.

✈ ✈ ✈ ✈

THAILAND

Thailand's courier industry seems to have been hard-hit by the Asia-wide economic downturn. Bridges Worldwide has closed down and, with the exception of the Jupiter flights handled by Siam Trans, courier operations seem to be on hold.

Note: All fares are quoted in Thai bhat (฿). Recently, the bhat was trading at approximately 42 to the US dollar.

OBC Carriers
1126/1 New Petchburi Road

Vanit Building #1, 16th floor, Room 1605
Bangkok 10400
(66) (2) 255-8590/1/2
(66) (2) 255-9593 (Fax)

In the past, OBC has offered courier service to Hong Kong and Singapore, but they have been hard hit by Thailand's economic woes. At press time, all flights had been suspended but there was some hope that flights to Singapore might resume in early 1999. When flights were operating, they were on Singapore airlines, at a fare of 4,000 bhat, for a stay of up to two weeks.

Contact Charlie Wong or Jintana Visanuvimol for information on the resumption of flights. If you're looking for their office, ask the taxi driver for the "Channel 3" building.

Siam Trans International Co. Ltd.

78 Kiatnakin Building
Bushlane, New Road
Bangkok 10500
(66) (2) 235-6741
(66) (2) 235-6751
(66) (2) 236-1042 (Fax)
email: skuntala@mozart.inet.co.th

This ground agent for Jupiter has been expanding its outbound operations to fill the void left by the disappearance of other Bangkok courier firms. Recently, their roster of flights looked like this:

Destination (Airline)	Departure Days	Length of Stay	Typical Fare
Chicago (JAL)	Monday – Saturday	Up to 60 days	฿20,000
Hong Kong (Thai)	Monday – Saturday	Up to 21 days	฿5,000
Los Angeles (JAL)	Monday – Saturday	Up to 60 days	฿18,000

Destination (Airline)	Departure Days	Length of Stay	Typical Fare
San Francisco (JAL)	Monday – Saturday	Up to 60 days	฿18,000
Singapore (Thai, Singapore)	Monday – Saturday	Up to 21 days	฿4,000

There are only a few courier flights each month to the U.S. destinations, and on a very erratic schedule. Call at least two weeks in advance to inquire about availability on these runs. Carry-on luggage only is allowed on the Singapore and Hong Kong runs, but couriers to the U.S. can check two bags in each direction.

STI sometimes has a need for couriers on short notice. If you're available, call the office and leave your name and number. They will call if something opens up.

Twenty kilos of luggage are allowed on STI's flights and you can book no more than two weeks in advance. Payment by credit card is possible, in person at their office. If you're going to their office, look for the blue and white street sign that says "Charoen Krung 30." Charoen Krung is Thai for "New Road" and Soi 30 is Captain Bush. Walk towards the river and the building will be on your left. Ask for the Operations Manager, Ms. Sirirat Nilphairojana, who speaks English.

LATIN AMERICA

Central America has largely disappeared from the list of courier destinations due in large part to the emergence of efficient cargo airlines operating out of Miami. These operators can fly roundtrips to the region overnight and offer a category of expedited air cargo that fills the niche once occupied by on-board couriers.

The countries of South America have a small air courier scene. Most courier runs from South America to Miami use returning couriers, who began their travel in the United States. However, because of booking peculiarities, there is an occasional need for a courier originating in South America. Thus, while courier opportunities from South America to the United States *do* exist, they are less numerous than runs from the United States.

ARGENTINA

Air Facility
Almafuerte 42, Barrio 1
Esteban Echeverria, Ezeiza
Prov. de Buenos Aires 1802
(54) (1) 480-9395
(54) (1) 480-9024 (Phone and Fax)

This branch of Air Facility is currently offering several courier runs, as follows:

Destination (Airline)	Departure Days	Length of Stay	Typical Fare
Miami (Aero. Arg.)	Monday – Saturday	Up to 30 days	US$500
Montevideo (Varig)	Monday – Saturday	same day turnaround	US$40–$50
Rio (Varig)	Tuesday – Saturday	Up to 15 days	US$150
Sao Paulo (Varig)	Tuesday – Saturday	Up to 15 days	US$150

The Montevideo run gets you to Uruguay at about 11:40 a.m. and you must return the same day at about 6:15 p.m. Apparently, most of the people who use this run are businessmen going for a short meeting; to them the nearly 70 percent savings in airfare is very attractive.

The Rio and Sao Paulo runs are served by one courier who can deplane in either city. Thus, on any given day, there will be a courier to Rio *or* Sao Paulo, but not to both.

Prices do not reflect departure taxes of US$23.50 from Argentina and $36 from Brazil.

Air Facility accepts bookings 20 days in advance only. Payment must be in cash only, at their offices; no credit cards. Ask to speak with Mariella Scarcella.

IMEX Airborne Express S.A.
Avenida Independencia 2182
Buenos Aires
(54) (1) 308-3555

This affiliate of International Bonded Couriers in Miami offers courier flights to Miami and Montevideo. Here is the current schedule:

Destination (Airline)	Departure Days	Length of Stay	Typical Fare
Miami (Aero. Arg.)	Monday – Friday	Up to 15 days	US$500
Montevideo (AeroArg, UA)	Occasionally	Call	Call

CHILE

I.B.C. Airborne Express
Antonia Lopez de Bello 173
Santiago
(56) (2) 737-7179
(56) (2) 737-7221 (Fax)
email: ibc.courier@chilnet.cl

This affiliate of International Bonded Couriers in Miami offers courier flights to Miami and Buenos Aires.

Destination (Airline)	Departure Days	Length of Stay	Typical Fare
Buenos Aires (Lan Chile)	Monday– Friday	Up to 30 days	US$100
Miami (Lan Chile)	Monday– Friday	Up to 30 days	US$450

Couriers are limited to carry on luggage only. Payment can be made either in U.S. dollars or Chilean pesos. The courier contact is Ana Maria Salas, who speaks very little English.

ECUADOR

Trans-Air Systems, Inc.

199

7264 NW 25th Street
Miami, FL 33122
(305) 592-1771
(305) 592-2927 (Fax)
email: tas@elink.net

Round-trip courier flights from Quito to Miami can be booked through Gloria Arauz at this office. The going rate is US$395, with a stay of 4 to 21 days. The flight is on American Airlines, with departures Tuesday through Saturday. If you'd like to stay for up to 30 days, the fare is US$550; up to 60 days US$595.

Once you have booked with Gloria, you can pay for your trip, in cash or traveler's checks, in US dollars, at Trans-Air's Quito office. The number there is (593) (2) 541-618. But remember, the booking must be made in Miami.

See the Miami listing for more information on Trans-Air System's policies and procedures.

GUATEMALA

Trans-Air Systems, Inc.
7264 NW 25th Street
Miami, FL 33122
(305) 592-1771
(305) 592-2927 (Fax)
email: tas@elink.net

Round-trip courier flights from Guatemala City to Miami can be booked through Gloria Arauz at this office. The going rate is US$280 to US$300, with a maximum stay of 30 days. The flight is on American Airlines. One-way trips, for United States residents only, are $260. If you'd like to stay for up to 60 days, the fare is US$320 to US$340; 90 days for US$485.

Once you have booked with Gloria, you can pay for your trip, in cash or traveler's checks, in US dollars, at Trans-Air's Guatemala office. The number there is (502) 331-8970. But remember, the booking must be made in Miami.

See the Miami listing for more information on Trans-Air System's policies and procedures.

Air Courier Glossary

Casual courier: A person who serves as a freelance courier from time to time. You and me!

Control the book: Very often, for any given courier run there will be one person or company who handles the details of booking couriers for that particular route. Other companies or booking agents may offer courier seats on the run but will always have to route the bookings through this person. This person is said to "control the book" for that particular courier run. It is very difficult if not impossible to determine who controls the book for any given run.

Courier pouch: Just a fancy name for the envelope containing the manifest (see below).

Co-loading: The practice of two or more courier companies sharing a single courier's baggage allotment.

Gateway: A city in which express shipments are consolidated for overseas shipment. For example, express shipments from Birmingham and Glasgow to New York would be consolidated in London, the gateway.

Line haul: Movement of air freight from one airport to another. Sometimes used to refer to the movement of freight from station to gateway airport to foreign airport to station.

GSA: (Abbreviation) General Sales Agent.

Hand carry: (Noun) Usually a special shipment requiring the use of an on-board courier on a run or to a destination that usually doesn't use on-boards.

Lock-out: The latest time at which a parcel can be accepted for courier shipment. Courier companies like to have the latest possible lock-out, so as to better serve their customers. That is why courier flights are generally the last flight of the day and why the courier tends to be the last person checked aboard the flight.

Manifest: The paperwork that accompanies a courier shipment. As a courier you will carry the manifest (usually) in a large, sealed envelope.

On-board courier: Another term for air courier.

Open the book: To begin booking couriers on flights. Usually used to describe the lead time in booking, as in the sentence, "We open the book three months before flight date."

Pouch: An individual bag containing envelopes and parcels being shipped with an on-board courier. Today, these "pouches" are actually large, semi-transparent, heavy-duty plastic bags. Some of them resemble Army duffel bags. A single pouch can hold about 70 pounds of cargo. Sometimes, the term "courier pouch" will be applied to the sealed envelope containing the shipment manifests that the on-board courier carries on his or her person during the flight.

Retailer: A freight company that sells expedited delivery services to the general public. Federal Express, DHL, TNT, as well as hundreds of smaller companies calling themselves "air courier services" are retailers. Some retailers also ship their own expedited cargo, either on chartered planes (Federal Express) or on regularly scheduled airlines as passenger's baggage (World Courier). Others turn their expedited shipments over to wholesalers (see below).

Returning courier: A courier on a flight that is taking him or her back to the city of origin.

Rostering: The process of filling available courier seats with couriers.

Run: A round-trip between Point A and Point B.

Station manager: The person in charge of an air courier company branch office; specifically, the person in charge of the actual shipping of cargo.

Wholesaler: A company that specializes in handling courier shipments for other companies. A wholesaler will negotiate special tariffs with the airlines based on the volume they bring in. A wholesaler like Halbart in New York may be putting courier bags from several different courier companies on each flight it books. Some wholesalers do some retailing on the side, others (like Halbart) are 100% wholesalers.

Destination Index

This city index gives you a quick way of finding out which courier companies go where you want to go. For each destination, I have listed the names of the courier companies that fly there and the city in which those companies are located (or from which they offer the flight). Refer back to the appropriate listing in the "International Air Courier Directory" for more information.

Not all the destinations listed here are mentioned in the text and some destinations require making connections. An asterisk (★) indicates that the company in question either offers the destination only occasionally or that it used to fly there but doesn't at present. Some of the defunct runs may be reinstated. I suspect, however, that many are things of the past. Still, hope springs eternal, as they say, and if you are hoping for a courier flight to Oslo or Berlin, this index will at least point you toward your most likely candidates.

Always remember that some destinations may not be available when you call, others may have been dropped, still others added. The courier business is the living embodiment of Toffler's dictum that "the only constant is change."

Amman, Jordan
    BATS (London)★
Amsterdam, Netherlands
    Air-Tech (NY)
    Halbart (Detroit)★
    Halbart (NY)
    Now Voyager (NY)
Athens, Greece
    Halbart (NY)★
    Now Voyager (NY)★
Auckland, New Zealand
    Air-Tech (NY)
    East-West (LA)
    East-West (NY)
    Jupiter (Sydney)★
    Now Voyager (LA)
    Now Voyager (NY)★
Bahrain City, Bahrain
    BATS (London)★
Bangkok, Thailand
    Air-Tech (NY)
    Air United (Singapore)
    Airtropolis (Singapore)
    BATS (London)★
    Bridges (HK)
    Bridges (London)★
    Bridges (Singapore)★
    Circle Concord (Singapore)
    East-West (NY)
    Fastlink (Tokyo)
    Halbart (NY)
    IBC (Chicago)★
    IBC (LA)
    IBC (SF)
    Jupiter (Chicago)
    Jupiter (HK)★
    Jupiter (LA)
    Jupiter (NY)★
    Jupiter (SF)
    Linehaul (HK)
    Now Voyager (Detroit)★
    Now Voyager (NY)
    UTL (Chicago)
    UTL (SF)
    Wholesale (Tokyo)★

Barcelona, Spain
    BATS (London)★
Beijing, China
    Air-Tech (NY)
    Bridges (London)
    East-West (NY)
    Jupiter (SF)★
    Linehaul (HK)★
    Now Voyager (NY)
    UTL (SF)
Berlin, Germany
    BATS (London)★
Boston, USA
    BATS (London)
Brisbane, Australia
    Air-Tech (NY)
    East-West (LA)
    East-West (NY)
Brussels, Belgium
    Air-Tech (NY)
    Halbart (Chicago)
    Halbart (NY)
    Jupiter (NY)★
    Now Voyager (NY)
    Travel HQ (Chicago)★
    World (NY)★
Budapest, Hungary
    BATS (London)
Buenos Aires, Argentina
    Air Facility (NY)
    Air Facility (Miami)
    Air-Tech (NY)
    BATS (London)
    Halbart (Miami)★
    I.B.C. (Santiago)
    IBC (Miami)
    Now Voyager (NY)
    Trans-Air (Miami)★
Cairns, Australia
    Air-Tech (NY)
    East-West (LA)
    East-West (NY)
Cairo, Egypt
    BATS (London)★

BATS (London)★
Circle Concord (Singapore)
Larnaca, Cyprus
   BATS (London)★
   Bridges (London)★
Lima, Peru
   Halbart (Miami)★
   Lima Services (Miami)
Lisbon, Portugal
   BATS (London)★
London, UK
   ACP (DC)
   ACP (LA)
   ACP (NY)
   ACP (SF)
   Aeronet (HK)
   Air-Tech (LA)
   Air-Tech (NY)
   Air United (Singapore)★
   Bridges (HK)★
   Dyna-Trans (HK)
   F.B. (Montreal)
   F.B. (Toronto)
   F.B. (Vancouver)
   Halbart (Boston)★
   Halbart (Chicago)
   Halbart (DC)★
   Halbart (LA)★
   Halbart (Miami)★
   Halbart (NY)
   IBC (LA)
   Jupiter (Chicago)★
   Jupiter (HK)★
   Jupiter (NY)
   Jupiter (SF)★
   Jupiter (Sydney)
   Linehaul (HK)★
   Now Voyager (NY)
   TNT (Auckland)
   Travel HQ (Chicago)
   UTL (SF)★
Los Angeles, USA
   ACP (London)
   Air United (Singapore)★
   BATS (London)★
   Bridges (London)★

Jupiter (HK)
Jupiter (London)★
Jupiter (Seoul)
Jupiter (Taipei)
Siam (Bangkok)
TNT (Auckland)
Madrid, Spain
   Halbart (Miami)★
   Halbart (NY)
   Now Voyager (NY)
Manchester, UK
   Linehaul (HK)★
Manila, Philippines
   Air-Tech (LA)
   Air-Tech (NY)
   Air United (Singapore)
   Airpak (Singapore)
   East-West (NY)
   Halbart (LA)
   Halbart (NY)
   IBC (LA)
   IBC (SF)
   Johnny (LA)
   Johnny (NY)
   Johnny (SF)
   Jupiter (SF)
   Linehaul (HK)★
   Now Voyager (NY)
   UTL (SF)
Mauritius
   BATS (London)
Melbourne, Australia
   ACP (London)
   Air-Tech (NY)
   East-West (LA)
   East-West (NY)
   Jupiter (LA)★
   Now Voyager (NY)
Mendoza, Argentina
   Trans-Air (Miami)★
Mexico City, Mexico
   Air Facility (NY)
   Air-Tech (NY)★
   BATS (London)
   Halbart (Chicago)★
   Halbart (Miami)★

IBC (Miami)
Now Voyager (NY)★
Trans-Air (Miami)★
Santo Domingo, Dominican Rep.
IBC (Miami)★
Sao Paulo, Brazil
Air Facility (Buenos Aires)
Air Facility (NY)
Air-Tech (NY)
Halbart (Miami)★
Now Voyager (NY)
Seattle, USA
BATS (London)
TNT (Auckland)★
Seoul, Korea
Air-Tech (NY)
All Nations (NY)
Bridges (London)
East-West (NY)
Halbart (NY)★
IBC (LA)
Jupiter (LA)
Linehaul (HK)★
Now Voyager (NY)
Shanghai, China
Air-Tech (NY)
East-West (NY)
Linehaul (HK)
UTL (SF)★
Singapore
Aeronet (HK)
Air-Tech (NY)
BATS (London)★
Bridges (HK)★
East-West (NY)
Fastlink (Tokyo)
Halbart (LA)★
Halbart (NY)
IBC (Chicago)★
IBC (LA)★
Jupiter (HK)
Jupiter (LA)
Jupiter (NY)
Jupiter (SF)★
Linehaul (HK)★
Now Voyager (Detroit)★

Now Voyager (NY)
OBC (Bangkok)★
Siam (Bangkok)
UTL (SF)★
Wholesale (Tokyo)★
Stockholm, Sweden
Halbart (NY)★
Now Voyager (NY)★
Sydney, Australia
ACP (London)
Air-Tech (LA)
Air-Tech (NY)
BATS (London)★
Bridges (HK)
East-West (LA)
East-West (NY)
Halbart (LA)
Halbart (NY)★
IBC (LA)★
Jupiter (HK)★
Jupiter (LA)★
Jupiter (London)★
Line Haul (London)★
Linehaul (HK)★
Now Voyager (LA)
Now Voyager (NY)
TNT (Auckland)★
Taipei, China
Air-Tech (NY)
Atlas Express (HK)★
Circle Concord (Singapore)
East-West (NY)
Halbart (LA)★
Halbart (NY)★
IBC (LA)★
Linehaul (HK)
Now Voyager (NY)
Tel Aviv, Israel
BATS (London)★
Courier Network (NY)
Halbart (NY)★
Now Voyager (NY)★
Tokyo, Japan
ACP (London)
Air-Tech (NY)
Air United (Singapore)★

Subject Index

Note: This subject index covers, primarily, Chapters 1 through 8 of the text. The names of companies listed in the "International Air Courier Directory" are also included here. To locate cities to which particular courier companies offer service, consult the "Destination Index," page 205.

Resources for the Intrepid Traveler
More Money-Saving Books from
"The Intrepid Traveler"

Home-Based Travel Agent —
How To Cash In On The Exciting NEW World Of Travel Marketing
Kelly Monaghan $29.95   ©1997, 1999   400 pages

Here's your chance to join the growing number of people who are earning good money and FREE trips just by sharing their love of travel with their friends and neighbors. Recent changes in the travel marketplace have created unparalleled opportunities for you to grab a piece of the $30,000,000,000 (*thirty billion*) travel market. What once was available only to a closed shop of "travel professionals" is now open to all.

YOU can become a Home-Based Travel Agent
— *INSTANTLY* —
and start earning $50, $100, $200 (*or more*)
for every trip you book!

This book reveals the secrets you need to:

- Open your own home-based travel agency.
- Avoid high start-up costs and limit your initial investment to pocket change.
- Book air travel, tours, cruises, hotels, and car rentals like a pro — and make money every time you do.
- Gain access to the airlines' sophisticated computerized reservations systems for just $15 a month.
- Buy a $1,200 airline ticket for $800 — and then resell it for whatever the traffic will bear.
- Work part-time for pocket change or forge a full-time career.
- Take tax-deductible cruises for a fraction of their normal cost.
- Get FREE trips from tour operators eager for your business.
- Earn FREE trips just by getting as few as four people to go with you.
- Get FREE magazines and travel info to help you build your business.

This is not a once-over-lightly treatment, but a COMPLETE, easy-to-use business system. You get detailed instructions on how to set up your business, how to legally earn a commission on all travel you sell (even to yourself!), how to make your first bookings, how to find (and keep) customers, how to take advantage of the many benefits available to travel professionals, and MUCH, MUCH MORE!

FREE, with every order of $30 or more — *Ticketing Ploys:*
How To Beat the Airlines at Their Own Game — a $4.00 value

Whether you just want to save some money on your own travel, start a fun part-time business out of your home, or become a six-figure, full-time travel agent, this book will tell you how. You'll save several times the cover price on the next family vacation you book using the tips contained in *Home-Based Travel Agent — How To Cash In On The Exciting NEW World Of Travel Marketing.*

"A definitive guide to getting in on the travel business. Kelly's book will tell you more than any of those mail-order deals about starting on a legitimate, part-time basis. And for lots less money."

Rudy Maxa, National Public Radio's 'Savvy Traveler'

"A gold mine of infomation for the independent contractor who wants to get his or her home-based travel business started on the right foot to success."

Gary M. Fee, Chairman, Outside Sales Support Network

"Finally, someone has written a travel agent book that tells it like it is. Kelly Monaghan's knowledge explodes off every page."

Donna M. Scherf, former Executive Director,
National Association of Commissioned Travel Agents

The Intrepid Traveler's Complete Desk Reference

Sally Scanlon and Kelly Monaghan
$16.95   ©1998   375 pages

What's an arunk? If you're flying into AUA, where are you going? The answers to these and thousands of other questions will be found in *The Intrepid Traveler's Complete Desk Reference*, an indispensable reference work for anyone who is really serious about travel. And if you're buying *Home-Based Travel Agent: How To Cash In On The Exciting NEW World Of Travel Marketing*, this book can help you look like a pro almost overnight! Here you'll find not just the definitions of common and obscure travel terms, but the kind of industry information a travel agent needs handy every day:

- The three-letter codes for every airport in the world that make booking reservations a snap.
- Codes for hotels and rental cars.
- An extensive directory of toll-free numbers for suppliers — airlines, hotels, rental cars, tour operators, and cruise lines.
- Complete listings of travel organizations and publications.
- Detailed information on how to get passports and visas.
- Time zones around the world at a glance.
- The currency of every country in the world.
- Sources of FREE travel information, across the nation and around the world.
- A complete glossary of travel-related terms, acronyms, and abbreviations.

FREE, with every order of $30 or more — *Ticketing Ploys: How To Beat the Airlines at Their Own Game* — a $4.00 value

A Shopper's Guide To Independent Agent Opportunities

Kelly Monaghan $39.95 ©1997 79 pages

There are a growing number of outfits offering you the chance to become a travel agent — overnight — and start reaping the many benefits available to the travel industry insider. But which one is right for you?

This information-packed Special Report, containing in-depth profiles of more than 60 companies, provides you with straightforward, *unbiased* information about the current crop of offerings.

In this no-holds-barred report, you will learn . . .

- How to evaluate an outside agent opportunity.
- What the glossy brochures *don't* tell you.
- How to find the best deals.
- The hard questions to ask before signing up with any company.
- Which companies charge *no sign-up fees whatsoever.* (And which ones charge the most!)
- What you get from each company. And just as important, what you *don't* get.
- The truth about travel industry benefits and why many companies offering outside agent opportunities don't want to tell you about it.

Get past the hype and the salesmanship. Get the straight information from someone who's been there. This insider information — not available anywhere else — will save you weeks of research time and let you narrow your search for an outside agent relationship that will work for you. It can also save you thousands of dollars in sign-up charges and annual fees.

**THIS INSIDE INFORMATION IS
NOT AVAILABLE ANYWHERE ELSE!**

***FREE**, with every order of $30 or more — Ticketing Ploys:
How To Beat the Airlines at Their Own Game* — a $4.00 value

Air Courier Bargains —
How To Travel World-Wide For Next To Nothing. (Seventh Edition)
Kelly Monaghan $14.95   ©1999   224 pages
If you borrowed this copy of *Air Courier Bargains*, why not get your own copy?

Consolidators: Air Travel's Bargain Basement
Kelly Monaghan
$7.95   © 1998   73 pages
In this exciting book, Kelly Monaghan unlocks the secrets of the world of
"consolidators" — travel specialists who buy huge blocks of seats from the
airlines at deep discounts and then pass those savings on to you. Lists over 300
consolidators across the U.S., both those who deal directly with the public and
those you can work with through your travel agent. Learn how to ...

- Get "super-saver" fares, even when the deadline has passed!
- Get an additional 5% off any flight you book yourself!
- Book by phone and receive your tickets in the mail!

Ticketing Ploys: How To Beat the Airlines at Their Own Game
Kelly Monaghan
$4.00   ©1998   Special Report
The airlines have a bewildering number of ticket rules, all designed to insure that
you pay a premium for your ticket. Savvy travelers have devised a number of ways
around these rules — back-to-back ticketing, hidden city ploys, bulk purchases,
and others. Some can get you in trouble if you're caught and should be avoided. But
the airlines' rules differ widely. What one airline says is a no-no is perfectly okay
with another. And many of the best ploys are perfectly legal. This Special Report
reveals the secret strategies for playing hardball with the airlines, while protecting
yourself against reprisals. A must-have for the serious business traveler or the travel
agent who *always* wants to get the best deal possible.
       FREE with your order of $30 or more! See coupon on last page.

How To Get A Job With A Cruise Line
Mary Fallon Miller
$14.95   ©1997   200 pages
WANTED! Adults of all ages, backgrounds, skills, and talents. To fill a broad
range of positions in the booming cruise line industry. If you have ever dreamed
of running away to work on the Love Boat, this book is like having a relative in
the cruise business. Mary Miller tells you precisely to whom, how, when, and
where to apply. Her inside know-how will save you hundreds of dollars, hours of
wasted time, and endless frustration. This all-new, completely revised fourth
edition contains the latest tips, techniques, policies, and contacts to make your
cruise line job search a snap.

         FREE, with every order of $30 or more — *Ticketing Ploys:*
         How To Beat the Airlines at Their Own Game — a $4.00 value

How To Get Paid $30,000 A Year To Travel (Without Selling Anything)

Craig Chilton

$24.95   ©1998   340 pages

Have you ever seen a Winnebago transported on the back of a truck? Or an ambulance? A hearse? A fire truck? Or a UPS truck? Chances are you never have. Craig Chilton, author of *HOW TO GET PAID $30,000 A YEAR TO TRAVEL (Without Selling Anything)*, will tell you why the delivery of recreational and specialty vehicles is America's greatest "sleeper" travel lifestyle. There are about 50,000 people throughout the USA and Canada who do this all the time, on a full-time or part-time basis, working for more than 1,000 manufacturers and transporter companies.

Here are some basic facts:

- In all states and provinces, all you need is an ordinary driver's license to deliver RVs. (Larger specialty vehicles require a chauffeur's license.)
- All companies provide full insurance coverage for vehicles and their drivers.
- All vehicles are new, so they're covered by manufacturer's warranty in case of breakdown.
- Companies pay all road expenses and return transportation, apart from earnings. (Earnings normally are based on the number of miles driven per trip.) Drivers who fly home normally get to keep all their frequent flyer miles.
- This lifestyle is nothing like trucking. No freight. Very few regulations. It's like getting paid to drive your own car.
- College students (18 and over) are needed during the summer months to supplement the regular work force. They typically earn $8,000-$12,000 during that season.
- 30 percent are retired people over age 65 who never worry about a "fixed income." (There's no upper age limit. As long as a person is a safe driver, he's in demand, due to his experience and maturity.)

Craig Chilton has appeared on more than 500 talk shows to inform the public about this profitable and fun lifestyle. This **NEW, COMPLETELY REVISED, 1998 EDITION** reveals Craig's system for maximizing this exciting lifestyle and lists more than 4,000 potential employers throughout the US, Canada, Europe, and Australia!

Who hasn't dreamed of getting paid to travel?
Now you can find out how.

A COMPLETE CAREER SYSTEM FOR JUST $24.95

FREE, with every order of $30 or more — *Ticketing Ploys: How To Beat the Airlines at Their Own Game* — a $4.00 value

Orlando's *Other* Theme Parks

What To Do When You've Done Disney

Kelly Monaghan

$16.95   **New** 1999 Edition   480 pages

There's a whole 'nother 'World' outside the 'Kingdom'

The Orlando area abounds in attractions of every sort — from thrill rides to pristine wilderness, paintball games to ballet. But general guidebooks have to devote so much space to Disney's multitude of attractions that the wealth of things to see and do outside Mickey's portals gets short shrift or not a single word. Now, *Orlando's OTHER Theme Parks* provides in-depth guidance to the abundance of other attractions in the greater Orlando area. Imagine:

- ❏ Nearly 100 pages devoted just to Universal Studios Florida.
- ❏ Over 50 pages on SeaWorld.
- ❏ New chapter on Islands of Adventure and CityWalk at Universal.
- ❏ Reviews of every non-Disney dinner attraction.
- ❏ Complete chapters on Cypress Gardens, Kennedy Space Center, Busch Gardens Tampa, Church Street Station, Gatorland, and Splendid China.
- ❏ Individual reviews of a legion of other attractions ranging from the area's spectacular miniature golf courses to airboat rides, amazing things to do and see — even the smallest go kart track.
- ❏ The "real Florida" of pristine wilderness walks and unspoiled canoe trails, just minutes from the tourist bustle.
- ❏ Extensive coverage of Orlando's burgeoning arts and sports scenes.
- ❏ Water parks, animal attractions, botanical gardens, museums, and more. **Plus** insider tips to help you get the most out of your Central Florida vacation.

All you need to find the sights and activities you'll enjoy most. And not a mouse in sight!

DON'T LEAVE FOR ORLANDO WITHOUT IT!

FREE, with every order of $30 or more — *Ticketing Ploys: How To Beat the Airlines at Their Own Game* — a $4.00 value

YOUR TICKET TO SAVING *BIG* MONEY ON TRAVEL

☐ **YES!** I want to succeed in my own home-based travel marketing business! Send me the Complete Home-Based Travel Agent System for just $69.95. (Counts as 3 books)

I prefer to order separately:

☐ *Home-Based Travel Agent: How To Cash In On The Exciting NEW World of Travel Marketing* $29.95

☐ *The Intrepid Traveler's Complete Desk Reference* $16.95

☐ *A Shopper's Guide To Independent Agent Opportunities* $39.95

☐ I need another copy of *Air Courier Bargains*, for just $14.95

☐ I want to see more than the Mouse! Send me *Orlando's OTHER Theme Parks* so that I'll be sure of getting the most out of my Central Florida trip. And it's just $16.95.

☐ I want to learn *How To Get Paid $30,000 A Year To Travel (Without Selling Anything)!* Send me Craig Chilton's blockbuster 1997 edition for just $24.95.

☐ I want to work on the Love Boat! Send me Mary Miller's *How To Get A Job With A Cruise Line* for just $14.95.

☐ I never want to pay full fare again. Send me *Consolidators: Air Travel's Bargain Basement* for just $7.95.

☐ My order totals more than $30, send me my **FREE** copy of *Ticketing Ploys.* ($4.00 if less than $30 or ordered by itself.)   **FREE**

Delivery Options: For regular postage (Special 4th Class Book Rate), add $3.50 for the 1st book and $.50 for each additional book ordered. Postage is $.75 for each Special Report. Allow 3 to 4 weeks for delivery. For faster UPS delivery, add $5.00 for the 1st book and $1.00 for each additional book ordered. For foreign delivery (except Canada), add 15% to "Total" for surface mail; for air mail costs fax 212-942-6687. **U.S. funds only.**	Book total
	NY tax (8.25%)*
	Regular postage
	UPS delivery
	TOTAL

*NY residents only

Name: _____

Address: _____
UPS can deliver only to street addresses (no P.O. boxes) in the continental US.

City: _____ State: _____ Zip: _____

Visa/MC/Amex: _____ Exp.: _____

Signature _____ Phone: _____

Make checks payable to:

The Intrepid Traveler • Box 438 • New York, NY 10034-0438
Fax credit card orders to 212-942-6687

Prices & availability subject to change without notice.

For more great books visit our web site
http://www.intrepidtraveler.com

IG7